Elephanta
THE CAVE OF SHIVA

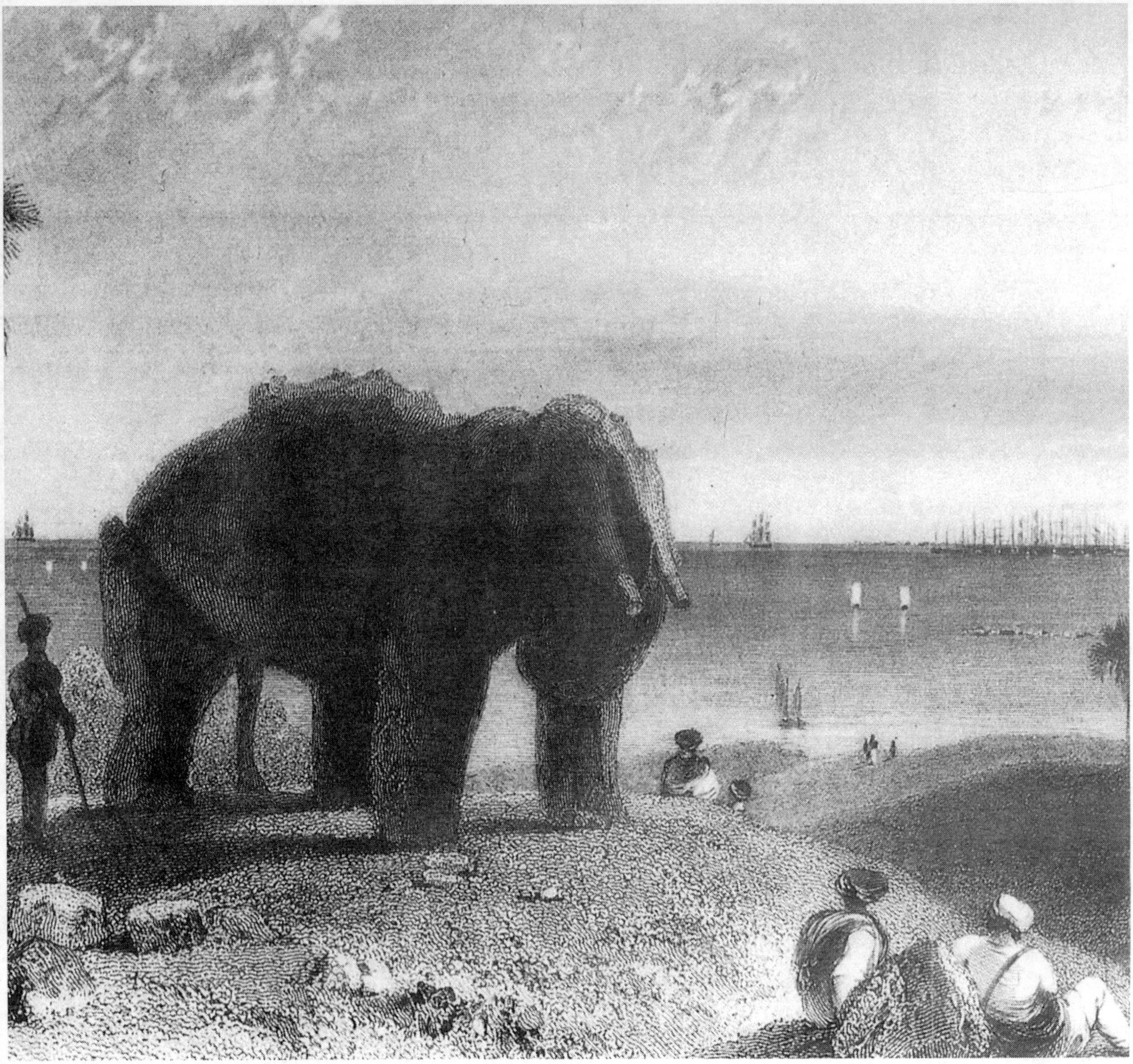

On the Island of Elephanta
Artist : W. Daniell; Engraving : R. Brandand

Elephanta

THE CAVE OF SHIVA

Photographs by Carmel Berkson

Essays by Wendy Doniger O'Flaherty, George Michell, and Carmel Berkson

MOTILAL BANARSIDASS PUBLISHERS
PRIVATE LIMITED ● DELHI

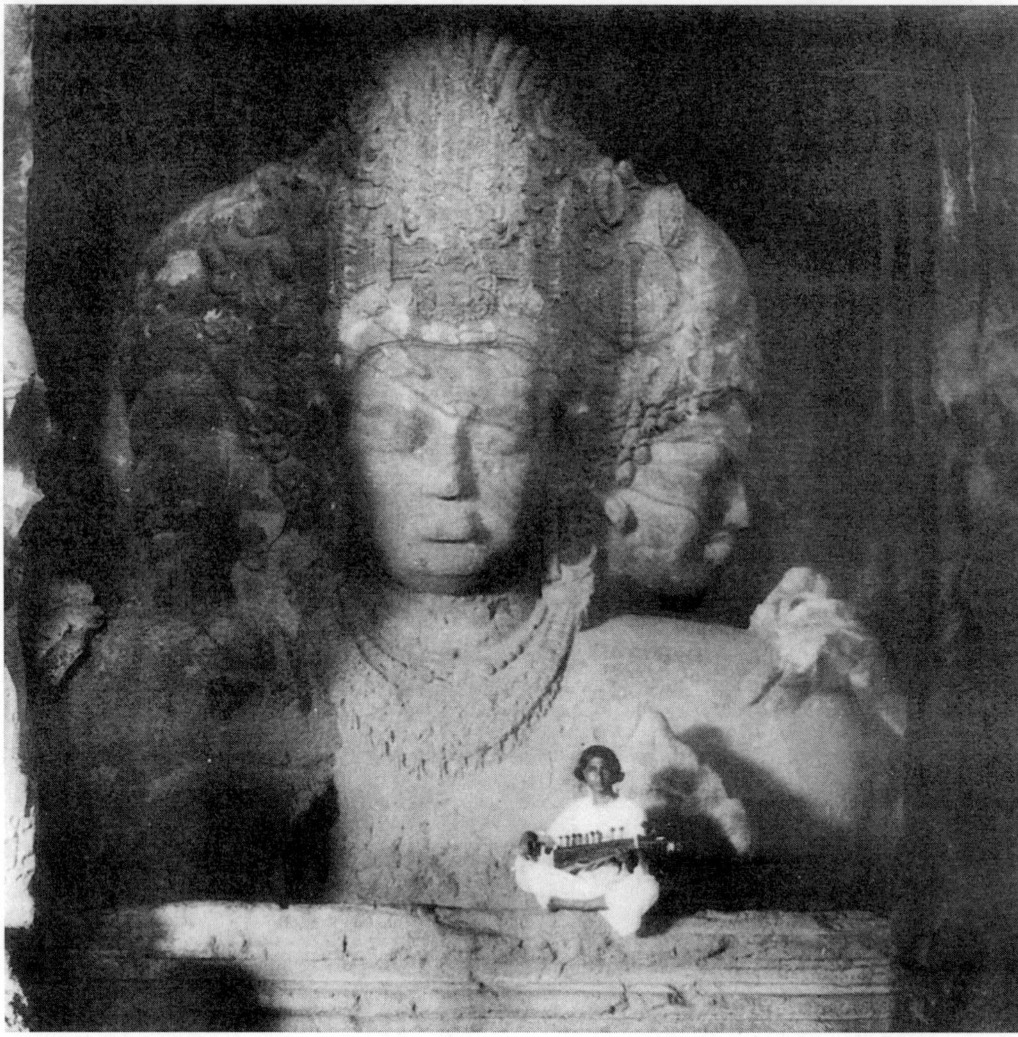

Sadashiva (Eternal Shiva), showing Timir Baran Bhattacharya playing the sarod in Elephanta in 1934 or 1935. Gift of Alice Boner to Carmel Berkson.

Dedication

FOR THIS VOLUME, Alice Boner had agreed to analyze the compositions of a number of the panels at Elephanta. Unfortunately, her proposed trip to Bombay in 1978 did not materialize, and although she later found it necessary to withdraw her offer to make the contribution, her enthusiastic support and encouragement continued throughout the period of preparation.

On April 13, 1981, Alice Boner died in Zurich at the age of 93. Along with her friends in India and around the world, we sorely miss having her with us, and therefore, with affection and deep appreciation of her fifty years of inspired work in India, we dedicate this volume to the memory of her valiant, devoted, and gentle spirit.

Acknowledgments

WENDY O'FLAHERTY's spontaneously generous response to the suggestion that we prepare a book about Elephanta and her indefatigable persistence in handling the details of publication while I was in India have not only made this volume possible but have provided a great amount of joy and excitement in its preparation.

I am grateful to Mitter Bedi. He advised and encouraged in regard to difficult problems of photography. Razak Banatwalla is responsible for printing the photographs.

Dr. M. N. Deshpande, retired Director General of the Archeological Survey of India, very kindly read the historical background material and suggested some additions, which have been incorporated.

C. B.

WENDY DONIGER O'FLAHERTY

Introduction

EVERYONE SHOULD VISIT Elephanta at least once in each lifetime. It breaks my heart to see the tourist droves milling about the Taj Mahal (a building that is, like a beauty contestant, pretty enough in its way, and perfect in all its dimensions, but not very exciting) and passing by this mysterious and spectacular island (named Elephanta by the Portuguese and best known by that name, though the natives call it Gharapuri). Because life is *not* perfect, this book is for those who cannot visit Elephanta—and for those who, having had the good fortune to visit it, wish to have a base on which to reconstruct their own memories of the place. It is not the same as the real thing, but through Carmel Berkson's extraordinary photographs it is possible to come far closer to the experience of Elephanta than I would ever have dreamed possible before I saw them.

These photographs achieve several different but interlocking purposes. First of all, they give one a feeling of the place. The visitor to Elephanta has just crossed the water for an hour or so (Pl. 1) in a small, sleepy launch, chugging modestly along out of Bombay harbor past large steamers and small fishing boats, through other harbors and islands, rocking in the hazy heat until the island of Elephanta draws near and the boat noses in and is made fast. Then there is a steep climb up more than a hundred steps, past trees heavy with blossom that exudes an almost sickly-sweet scent, alive with birds and monkeys, past vendors selling postcards and baubles, until one reaches the top—the caves (Pl. 2).

Here one first encounters the dramatic alternation of light and dark that makes the caves so disquieting, and so difficult to photograph. Carmel Berkson's pictures capture the feeling of being in cool shade surrounded by painful sunlight, of gazing into dark recesses while still blinded by the natural light a few feet away, of slowly beginning to adjust to the strange light that seems to come out of some of the inner recesses and corners. Several of the pictures, especially when viewed for several minutes, recreate the feeling of being slightly off-balance, slightly out of kilter with the axis of gravity, a feeling that falls upon you when you lose touch with the planes outside and accept the cave's own definitions of up and down, the irregular foreshortenings and tilts of the eye and the mind. This disorientation is closely akin to the one so brilliantly described by E. M. Forster in

A Passage to India, the magic of the caves that so deeply disturbs not only the brittle Miss Quested but even the saintly Mrs. Moore.

The second achievement of this set of pictures is to preserve with remarkable clarity and beauty the overall composition of the great paneled bas-reliefs. They have been documented before in several standard works on Indian art, but never so well. For the task is not nearly so straightforward as one might think: the light is so irregular, changing significantly in each space of a few inches and each passing of a few seconds, and the panels are so large, that it is a matter of art, not science, to find a time of day and a time of year when the angle of the sun, and the interplay of shadows, and the refraction of the other angles of the caves make it possible to see the whole panel clearly. Artificial light flattens, distorts, and destroys the warm texture of the stone; more important, it cancels out the light that comes *out of* the sculptures, an extraordinary radiance that is uncannily captured by these photographs. Alice Boner, whose ill health unfortunately kept her from completing the preface that she so much wished to write for this volume, remarked in a letter to Carmel Berkson, "Your last batch of photographs from Elephanta . . . are the most wonderful of all. Although they mostly are of the most brutally mutilated panels, they are radiating the intimate sacred atmosphere of these caves inside the mountain, which goes to the heart."

There is also the problem of angles. The relief is so deep that the shapes change sometimes beyond recognition when one moves just a few inches forward or to one side. There is no single "accurate" angle by which to view the panel, though the most straightforward is from the center and as close as possible without cutting off any of the edges. This angle does not, however, correspond to the "reality" of the image, to the hard-core scientific or historic essence ("Wie es eigentlich gewesen ist"); to view the caves is to plunge into a drama like *Rashomon*, where every new angle is entirely different and entirely true. By presenting several different angles in series, Carmel Berkson gives the reader of this volume the impression one would have in moving slowly past the panel, lingering, seeing a particular figure first in profile and then full face, first in detail and then, stepping back, in the setting of the group in which it is carved; and then, stepping forward again and to the side, from a different profile; and perhaps, bending down, from the underside. The result is not unlike some of Picasso's early attempts to capture both the profile and the full face of a woman at the same time; or a movie montage in which one sees the actor's face close up, superimposed on his body in a landscape. This is far more than an alternation between details and full shots; it is a matter of letting the eye move in and out and around those particular points of light and texture that the general view draws one into, and of recognizing when a new angle reveals a new scene sufficiently different to merit a separate record.

Finally, Carmel Berkson's choice of subjects to photograph in detail reveals an eye sensitive not only to beauty but to humor, character, myth, idiosyncrasy, puzzles, and religion. It is a mature, loving eye. The strange little things that one might miss even on a visit made in person are highlighted and made important; grotesque dwarfs, elegant fingers, baroque curls of hair, funny pots, bit players in the great dramas, all come alive out of the stone in these pages. For, thanks to her mastery of the techniques of time-exposure, telescopic lens, high mountings, and wide-angle lens, as well as to her eagle eye, she has captured in these photographs many things that one cannot see *except* with a camera (in addition to preserving those things that one can see with the eye and also with the camera)—details hidden behind other things, blocked by pillars, too far away or too high up, wrapped in the shadow of an adjacent blinding light. She has also managed to capture, in her deep portraits of the alleys and doorways of the cave, the peculiar vision of Elephanta (as of several other Indian caves). For, in contrast with the great structural temples that seem to grow right up *out* of the landscape, so that from the distance one may mistake them for hillocks or clumps or trees, the caves grow down *into* the land; they then impose upon the person inside a different view of the rest of the world, the world outside, seen differently when framed by the portals of the cave, and seen differently ever after.

The pictures are the true *raison d'être* of this book, and the text is provided merely to make them more accessible and meaningful to the reader. Carmel Berkson's own essay supplies the essential historical background as well as her own view of the meaning of the style of the sculptures. Her bibliographic survey indicates the places where one might look for other people's answers to some of the questions and speculations that arise in the course of her essay; the bibliography also demonstrates how remarkably little has been written about Elephanta. George Michell brings his unique combination of talents to play—training as an architect, long intimacy with Indian temple sculpture, and a rare ability to say precisely what he means—to suggest ways in which the overall structure of the cave may have been infused with deep meanings that encompass and enhance the particular meanings of each sculptural group. And I have tried to present some of the mythological insights and theological attitudes that may have been in the minds of the sculptors so many centuries ago and that are still "good to think with," as Claude Lévi-Strauss says, when we encounter this powerful and passionate view of the world.

Notes on Terminology

Major Terms

Elephanta (Gharapuri). Because the Portuguese found a monolithic stone elephant at the docking area when they first arrived on the island, they named it Elephanta (*Frontis.*). The island is known to its inhabitants as Gharapuri, which may mean "city of priests," but we have used the term most familiar to other Indians as well as to Western scholars.

Eternal Shiva (Sadashiva). The main icon of Shiva with three heads has been called by many names. Collectively the faces are regarded as five emanations from the formless, unmanifested Para-Brahma, the Supreme Principle. Texts of medieval iconography identify and give details about the five heads, which are said to represent the five elements (ether, air, fire, water, and earth). Stella Kramrisch has identified the three heads as Aghora, Tatpurusha, and Vamadeva, with Sadyojata implied at the back and Ishana (the first and highest manifestation) at the top. The statue has been referred to as Mahesha, Mahadeva, Trimurti, and Sadashiva (Eternal Shiva), which is at present the term preferred by Indian art historians.

Shiva Dancing in Lalita. Although this panel is generally known as Nataraja (King of Dancers), the application of this term to Elephanta has been questioned. C. Sivaramamurti, in conversation, explained that the term Lalita, which connotes grace or charm, does not refer to the symbolism of creation and destruction in Shiva's dance but is merely the correct term for the position in which the figure is posed, as described in the textbook on dancing (*Natya Shastra*).

Two Axes. The two major axes—from east to west, leading to the *linga* in the shrine, and from north to south, leading to Eternal Shiva—define the directions of the cave. For centuries, puzzled observers have speculated as to which axis was primary, and the contributors to this volume are still continuing to think, and disagree, about this problem.

MINOR TERMS	apsara	celestial maiden
	bhakta	devotee
	caitya	assembly hall
	caturmukha	four heads (applied to the four doorways in the shrine)
	chakra	disc (weapon of Vishnu)
	chowri	fan(bearer)
	darshana	personal manifestation
	dvarapala	doorkeeper
	gajahasta	arm positioned like the trunk of an elephant
	gana	dwarf, servant of the god Shiva
	hamsa	swan, vehicle of Brahma
	linga	phallus
	makara	mythical beast, composite of lion, crocodile, peacock, pig, and elephant; vehicle of Varuna
	makuta	diadem, headdress
	mandapa	hall
	matrika	mother
	maya	illusion
	nirguna	unqualified, latent aspect of god
	pancha-mukha	five heads
	pitha	pedestal, base for *linga*
	pradakshina	circumambulation
	prasada	food for gods
	rishi	holy man
	saguna	specific, inflected personified form of god
	shakti	power
	stupa	Buddhist relic mound
	tandava	destructive dance of Shiva
	tapas	ascetic penances
	torana	gateway
	vidyadhara	flying figure, celestial being
	vihara	monastery
	yakshi(a)	local vegetation deity, male and female
	yugas	four ages of the world
SHIVA'S ASPECTS	Aghora	fierce
	Tatpurusha	transcendent
	Vamadeva	graceful

The Gods Appearing in the Panels

		The vehicle
Agni	fire god	ram
Brahma	the creator	*hamsa*, swan
Candra	the moon	
Ganesha	elephant-headed son of Shiva	rat
Indra	king of the gods	Airavata, elephant
Karttikeya	war god son of Shiva	peacock
Parvati	the goddess	
Shiva		Nandi, bull
Varuna	god of waters, guardian of the western quarter	*makara*, composite animal
Vishnu		Garuda, eagle

Others

Bhagiratha	a king
Bringhi	a devotee of Shiva
Himalaya	king of the mountain, father of Parvati
Nila	elephant associate of the demon Andhaka

Names of the Panels

Entering at the east, which was the original entrance, starting with Ravana, the visitor should make a circumambulation (*pradakshina*) around the shrine in this order:

Terms used in this study	*Traditional Sanskrit terms*
Ravana (lifting Kailasa)	Ravana
Gambling Scene	Umamaheshvara
Androgyne	Ardhanarishvara
Eternal Shiva	Sadashiva (Mahadeva, Maheshvara, Maheshamurti)
(Descent of the) Ganges	Gangadhara
Marriage (of Shiva and Parvati)	Kalyanasundara
(Impaling the demon) Andhaka	Andhakasuravadha
Shiva dancing (in Lalita)	Nataraja
Lord of Yogis	Yogishvara or Mahayogishvara
Karttikeya	Karttikeya
Ganesha	Ganesha
Mothers	Matrikas

Elephanta

CARMEL BERKSON

The Historical Context and Evolution of Style at Elephanta

SINCE PALEOLITHIC TIMES man has interred the dead in caverns deep in the earth and in natural rock shelters closer to the surface. By the eleventh dynasty, Middle Kingdom (c. 2050 B.C.) in Egypt, the art of excavating rock tombs had already become highly refined as stone and metal tools were sharpened and strengthened for the purpose. Tombs and sanctuaries were excavated in Malta, Sardinia, and the Hittite kingdom in the second millennium B.C. and in Phrygia and Scythia in Anatolia and in Persia in the sixth century B.C. Outstanding examples, carved in the early centuries A.D., are in Israel, Jordan, and Iran.

When the Mauryan Empire came into contact with Persia in the third century B.C., Indian artists seem to have borrowed the technical skills needed to express a particular Indian aesthetic. The first group of excavations appeared in the Barabar and Nagarjuni hills in Bihar. With an offshoot in Orissa, the art soon spread to the Deccan, where in the basalt and other trap rocky hillsides of the Western Ghats an extraordinary burst of building activity continued for a millennium, with the result that there are over a thousand caves in the area. With the introduction of such an amount of diversity, originality, and multiplicity of form, the Indians carried the art of rock architecture to summits beyond the wildest imagination of their predecessors. The early caves were Buddhist assembly halls (*caityas*) and square or rectangular monasteries (*viharas*).

During this long period architects experimented with the organization of the excavated space within the mountain, with aniconic and iconic representations, with columniation and with the incorporation of associative sculpture. From the beginning the caves were designed by experienced, proficient craftsmen with extreme precision based on complicated mathematics. Those who had been carpenters in wood adapted their skills to stone carving, and goldsmiths soon learned to do the finishing work.

These new skills of carving in stone gave the art of sculpture considerable impetus. At first artists executed in stone edict pillars with elaborate capitals, pillars in Asoka's palace, gigantic local fertility deities (*yakshis* and *yakshas*), and the railings and gateways of the Buddhist monuments teeming with sculptured bas-reliefs. These are at Bharhut, Bodh Gaya, Sanchi, Jaggayyapeta and Amaravati. By the first centuries of the Christian era, Brahmanical image worship had long since replaced Vedic sacrifice, the image of the Buddha and Jain Tirthankaras became popular objects of worship, Kushan emperors and nobles commissioned their own images and portraits, and *stupa* building continued at Amaravati and Nagarjunakonda and related sites. At this time, schools of sculpture at Mathura, at Sarnath, and in Gandhara, and their provincial offshoots became important centers for the development of iconographical and stylistic modes to suit the various ideologies. At a seminal workshop at Samalaji many of the fundamentals of the various aspects of the Hindu pantheon and the particulars of its iconography were evolved or expressed in stone for the first time. Also the inflorescent unfolding of forms of Shiva out from a central axis of figures in the Parel monolith near Bombay already hinted at some of the Elephanta style, techniques, and boldness of spirit.

As for the incorporation of sculpture into the caves, major figures were confined to the outside of the early Buddhist caves, for example at Karla, Kanheri, and Pitalkhora. But later at Ajanta and at the Buddhist caves of Ellora and Aurangabad, after the fifth century, remarkably complex arrangements of sculpture within the interior of the main hall (*mandapa*) and especially in the shrines created awesome sacred environments. Large figures of Bodhisattvas and guardian figures or doorkeepers (*dvarapalas*) at these sites find their counterparts at Elephanta.

Panels carved on monastery walls whether for didactic purposes or to be used for worship were introduced at places like Bhaja and Kondane. At Nasik many early panels depict the Buddha and Bodhisattvas. At Khambalida in Saurashtra, two large panels flank the doorway of a cave carved during the Satavahana period with large guardian figures surrounded with profuse carvings.

In the fifth century the art was augmented at the early Hindu temples of Deogarh, Bhitargaon, and those erected under Vakataka influences as exemplified by sculptures preserved at Paunar Ashram of Shri Vinoba Bhave near Nagpur and at the Hindu rock excavations at Udayagiri. Many of the caves at Kanheri have elaborate reliefs. Caves 17 and 26 at Ajanta mark a definite shift away from the arts of painting in the direction of sculptured panels, which later flowered at Aihole, Badami, Aurangabad, and Ellora.

The reader who is interested in the dynastic patronage and relative chronology of the caves of this period is referred to the bibliography.

The island of Elephanta had for centuries been a commercial, military, and religious center, and it still has traces of the early Buddhist culture. With the resurgence of the Brahmanical religion the great cave, dedicated solely to Shiva, exploded into existence. Walter Spink's theory that the cave was constructed by the Kalachuri king Krsnaraja in the mid-sixth century is generally accepted.

The plan of the cave can be traced directly back five or six hundred years to the simple excavated Buddhist monastery in India, with its cells for living aligned along three walls of a square court. In many cases a veranda was built at the front entrance, which was left open. With the appearance of the large assembly halls accommodating many people for worship, the need arose for more living space. Examples of Buddhist monasteries built in the early centuries A.D. can be found at Ajanta, Caves 12 and 13, at Bhaja, Kanheri, Bedsa, and Junnar without columns, and at Kondane and Pitalkhora with columns. Caves 3, 8, and 15 at Nasik show an increasing complexity, with larger hall space and a greater number of cells.

As the worship of the figure of the Buddha began to be encouraged with the development of Mahayana Buddhism, a shrine was introduced to house this image, replacing cells at the center of the back wall. All the later monasteries at Ajanta, Ellora, and Aurangabad are built in this way. These more elaborate monasteries at Ajanta lead us directly toward Elephanta. The hall columns, varying in number, are positioned in a square formation which permits circumambulation between the columns and the cell walls. In Cave 6, lower floor, sixteen columns are evenly disposed in the hall. This begins to resemble the plan at Elephanta where the side walls are eliminated and replaced by verandas.

In Cave 2 at Ellora, the side cells have also been transformed into panels with Buddha images, and, as at Elephanta, the capitals of the columns are shaped like a closed lotus. Though we do not know which cave is earlier, we can see the connections.

The same families of craftsmen and sculptors were employed in the construction of Brahmanical and Buddhist shrines. At Jogeshvari near Bombay, the idea of a square shrine is linked to an earlier structure, the fifth-century temple at Deogarh, which is in itself a square sanctuary situated atop a square terrace. Three doors replace the wall panels of Deogarh. Today, within the four-doored (*caturmukha*) shrine, the priest at Jogeshvari still moves ritually from door to door chanting and ringing his bell.

But the walls of the halls at Jogeshvari are solid. It was the architect of Elephanta who first conceived the idea of opening the temple to the outside on three sides, permitting and encouraging nuanced transitions from light to dark and back again. Sunlight entering from so many directions and changing from moment to moment and season to season defines the nature of the experience here (and later at Dhumar Lena cave, Ellora): profuse alterations in the shadings of light are more integrally involved with the space and mass of the cave here than anywhere else. Keeping the idea of the Buddha shrine in the back wall and the original front veranda, the architect replaced the side cells and walls of the monastery with verandas, thus, in an ingenious way, providing wall space for nine sculptured panels.

No doubt the cave was the creation of an unknown genius, a master architect who, having thoroughly absorbed and assimilated the magnificent contributions of his predecessors in the dual traditions of the carving of independent freestanding sculpture and rock-cut architecture, produced a monument which introduced a whole new world of form quite distinct from any previous achievement.

Continuities from the past can be traced in composition, iconography, puranic content, spatial arrangement, style, and the use of mathematically precise measurements for figures and architecture. Some qualities in the Ajanta frescoes reappear in Elephanta, transformed of course as required by the different medium. There were, however, few precedents which anticipated or can explain the prolific outpouring of multifarious form and the unique and concentrated structural dynamics in each of the panels, or their mutual relationships with one another and with the mass and space within the cave.

In its ultimate synthesis of infinitely diversified and mobile forms with new modes of expressing metaphysical conceptions of the deity, the achievements of the Elephanta artists represent an abrupt departure from the past. So much sculpture, arranged in panels placed as stations along a circumambulatory path had never been carved in one place before.

Writing about Buddhist images, Coomaraswamy (*Selected Papers*, Princeton, 1977) states:

> Icons, serving as reminders of the great moments of the Buddha's life and participating in his essence are to be regarded as "stations" at the sight of which a "shock" or "thrill" may and should be experienced by monk or layman. . . . In the deepest experience that can be induced by a work of art . . . our very being is shaken to its roots.

How true this is of Elephanta! A great effort was made to shape a permanent universe out of physical matter to capture an eternal unchanging condition—permanence, immutability, and fixity—and simultaneously to depict the nature of physical reality—impermanence, mutability, fluctuation, and all the torture of phenomenal existence. The worshiper at Elephanta is brought into a newer, more concentrated, and most complex vortex, where packed energy is captured in the bowels of the earth, violent and dissonant forces crash and clash in tumultuous and passionate confrontations of opposing forces, often unresolved and often not coming to rest. Flux as the nature of the ever-changing universe is what is primarily reflected. The serious devotee however does ultimately grasp the whole, thereby achieving a sense of reintegration, quiescence, and transcendence.

So major are the differences in style in the various panels that it is tempting to try to arrange them into familiar categories which imply a definite passage of time for their development. It is however less valuable to think in terms of classifications such as "archaic" or "classical" than to examine and appreciate the nuances existing in all types of configurations and in those facets and combinations which, united, constitute a multiform world which defies categorization.

A momentous break with the past resulted from the new strivings toward the incorporation of three-dimensional sculpture into the walled panel. These experiments naturally led to innovative schemes of organizing the space, volume, and depth. Although in the Buddhist caves at Ajanta, Aurangabad, and Ellora the artists had created a shrine filled to the bursting point with three-dimensional figures, none of the more or less contemporary Hindu panels either at Udayagiri, Aihole, Badami, or Ellora was conceived as shrinelike. Bas-relief was basic to these sites, but at Elephanta the major emphasis was on the movement away from relief toward chamberlike environments. This synthesis of freestanding sculpture, shrine, and wall was an important contribution to the history of art.

Our task is to study the many modes which the artist employed to accomplish this. Combinations of flatter and more rounded dimensions appear together within the same panel, but there is a general tendency away from relief. The sequence of the panels in regard to development into depth might be arranged as follows: 1) Ganges (Pl. 44) 2) Marriage (Pl. 51) 3) Androgyne (Pl. 31) 4) Shiva Dancing (Pl. 64) 5) Lord of Yogis (Pl. 68) 6) Andhaka (Pl. 59) 7) The Gambling Scene 8) Ravana (Pl. 70) and 9) the final dénouement: the Eternal Shiva (Pls. 39, 40) and 10) the four-door shrine (Pls. 4, 5).

As for the relationship of volume to the background and the level of depth penetration into the mountain rock, major differences exist between the panels, and we cannot determine the amount of time it took to make the transitions, say from the relatively flat and frontal carving of the figure of Ganges Shiva—followed by gradual changes in other panels—to its opposite, the Ravana panel, where the entire group of figures which includes the striding dwarf (*gana*), Bhringi (the skeletal devotee) (Pl. 70), Shiva and Parvati (Pl. 71) are completely separated from the concave background. They are carved in the round almost like freestanding sculpture. In the Gambling Scene panel the figure of Uma (Parvati) (Pl. 28) also represents a unique advance in this respect. Nor can we say definitely that the Ganges panel does stand chronologically before Ravana, although instinct tells us that this is so. Shiva in the Andhaka panel (Pls. 60, 61) is also much removed from the background, in a different way. Though the back is attached to the wall, the figure is totally three-dimensional. Observing the transitions and differentiations within each panel and from one panel to another makes a fascinating study; there is no definite progression, but only a combination of general tendencies.

Many new techniques were employed in this journey into the three-dimensional. Progress was not always straightforward or direct. For example, in the Ganges panel, Bhagiratha's kneeling figure is in three dimensions, isolated entirely from the background, but it is only a tentative attempt since this figure is not integrated with the others. In the same panel, Shiva's two right shoulders have scant volume and are flat compared to the magnificent serialization in the Andhaka panel, where the shoulders are placed one behind the other, a rhythmic cluster of bulbous, vegetative forms which transport the eye back into the depths of the rock.

In some panels two distinct tendencies are juxtaposed within the same frame. Certain figures which appear to have a minimal amount of three-dimensionality from the frontal view change radically from other perspectives. For example, in the Androgyne panel (from a seat at the doorstep of the adjacent cell) (Pl. 33) one sees that the sculptors have excavated deeply into the rock, thereby releasing a three-dimensional figure on the male side of Shiva. This view enables us to move backward toward the ground with the rhythms of the head of Nandi and Shiva's graceful arms one behind the other. The preparation of a spatial environment for a rounded figure to occupy is an invention which deserves attention as an important turning point; in fact, such moments in the history of art are rare, and this view, which is hardly ever seen, is probably one of those great moments. The definition of space depends greatly on the fact that Nandi is carved—hump, head, and forequarters (Pls. 31, 32, 36)—in a position perpendicular to the wall, a position borrowed from freestanding sculpture at Samalaji and from earlier coins. The way has now been paved for the alliance of freestanding sculpture with a bas-relief panel conception; though attached to the wall, the statue is gradually being released from its dominance. Later(?) the artist virtually extricates the figure from its involvement with and dependence upon the background.

Another astonishing advance can be observed in the lower portion on the west side of the Gambling Scene panel. The group of three playful figures, which in Rameshvara Cave at Ellora are carved entirely in bas-relief, are here placed in a zigzag movement toward a deeply carved background, with Nandi the bull again perpendicular to the ground.

In some panels action takes place primarily superimposed upon or emerging out of the back wall (the Ganges, Androgyne, Shiva Dancing, Andhaka, and Lord of Yogis panels). In Shiva Dancing and in the Lord of Yogis the side walls are flat but denuded of figures. The Marriage panel has its side figures turned toward the center, but all action takes place within a rather shallow space from front to back. In the Gambling Scene panel and then even more markedly in the Ravana panel, the guardians (Pls. 72, 75), back against the side walls, exist within very ample space. They turn toward the main figures and gaze outward. In conjunction with the concavity of the background, the environment has now become chamberlike.

Some of the panel figures appear to be stationary and independent of one another, but at the same time each of these figures is performing different functions simultaneously, and each can take its place in a group which is itself nonstatic. These conditions arise primarily in the Ganges, Marriage, Gambling Scene, and Ravana panels, although the Eternal Shiva is subject to some of the same principles in the interrelationship of the three heads and its position in the south wall.

How are we to read these panels? We experience ambivalent reactions all the time. A single figure may unite with an adjacent one to form an independent group, or the very same figure can be seen in conjunction with another on its opposite side. These groups are comprised of two or more figures, each functioning in relation to one or another of the figures closest to it. This results in an elusive, unsettling, variable, constant interplay of forms.

For example, Parvati can be seen in the Marriage panel first as the partner of Himalaya (Pl. 53), or again as the partner of Shiva (Pl. 54), who could have stood entirely independently. Or the three figures can be seen as a group (Pl. 55). Or Himalaya forms a group with the fan bearer (*chowri*) with or without Parvati, the fan bearer with the moon (Candra) (Pl. 52), etc. The ambiguous effects are caused by the more or less equal distribution of weights in relation to the surrounding space.

These are seemingly inexhaustible relationships that activate the panel; what seemed at first to be a static situation becomes a field of continuous flux and change. The panel never comes to rest but is dominated by constant movement, an interminably continuous transmutation of shifting forms. Each panel is a composite of many different assemblages in which the spectator is given the dizzying freedom to do his own organizing. Different groupings simultaneously affect the viewer; everything happens at the same time. To fix any group, one must artificially limit one's field of vision, as with a camera. We try to make a conceptual integration of the diverse and changing configurations, not unlike watching a carousel in motion, which however is a more ordered situation. These shifting groupings are inherently stable because they can be captured by the camera and are self-contained, but at the same time, they are dynamic because they are easily transformable.

At times the groupings ignore the frame and move out from its confines to combine with attracting elements outside the frame. Sometimes, therefore, the frame is an arbitrary device, an artificial and weak border which is submissive to more forceful magnetic pulls that are at work. The panels of the south wall function in this manner as a totality. The guardian and dwarf between the Eternal Shiva and the Ganges Shiva (Pl. 45) unite with Shiva alone or with Shiva's own dwarf and Parvati (in the Ganges panel).

In the case of the Marriage panel, this process also reflects the mood of the narrative. Parvati as Shakti is the agent of transformation, the primary mover; it was she who fought her parents and performed penances to determine her own fate. While still being protected by her father, Himalaya, she is also at the same time in the process of being transformed from daughter to wife. This is indicated by her turning figure, with left shoulder forward, hip poised in voluptuous extension. She is also at the point of leave-taking.

Some of the panels are arranged on a more or less vertical-horizontal axis; in some (the Ganges, Marriage, Lord of Yogis, and the Androgyne panels) verticality dominates; in others (the Gambling Scene and Ravana panels) horizontality dominates. This is true of the view from the front. A shift in the spectator's view, however, completely and astonishingly changes the whole composition and disrupts the expectations built up in front of the panel. For example, in the Marriage panel, if we shift to the rim of the veranda, standing near the corner, we observe that we are now looking at a row of horizontally placed figures (Pl. 52) which appear to be more or less the same size (this picture taken with wide-angle lens distorts the size of Shiva). The verticality is gone. Shiva, Parvati, the fan bearer, and Candra are seen, but none of these figures dominates. When the spectator shifts, the composition changes. Again from a view at the top of the stairs of the south door of the shrine, the very same panel takes on a third aspect with a new compositional structure, very different from the others. A series of forms moves in a counter-clockwise direction with Shiva and Parvati now having central positions. Starting with Brahma, the eye moves upward to the fan bearer, Vishnu, the flying figures (*vidyadharas*), etc. The circular tendency is not at all noticeable from the front. Shifting our view to the front of the Ganges panel, standing before the Eternal Shiva, we see the horizontal line of figures. In the Gambling Scene and Ravana panels, similar effects can be observed. When we examine the Ajanta frescoes, keeping in mind the play of forces at Elephanta, we find that some common aesthetic principles are expressed at both the great sites.

Though in antecedent works we might trace a kind of unfolding, nevertheless nothing in the history of Indian art has really prepared us for the marvelous play of dynamic forces in the Shiva Dancing and Andhaka panels. With the east wing shrine guardian figure (Pl. 10) and then the Shiva in the Gambling Scene (Pl. 28) panel acting as transitional figures, an entirely new style emerges which depends on the fact that the major forms are aligned only along diagonal axes, a total rupture from the previous vertical-horizontal direction. This is accompanied by a marked expansion of volume. Shiva's form is detached from the wall, a powerfully thick mass of dense stone.

The figure of Shiva Dancing has been violently disengaged from the still primarily flat background on its right side; the shoulder is thrust forcefully forward, backed by a series of other rounded shoulders (Pl. 65), so that the upper portion of the body turns toward the north entrance. Obliquely juxtaposed, its primary masses move in contrasting directions at different planar levels. The dance theme encourages the sculptor to make experiments in the shape and relationships which the body parts assume at their most extremely mobile moments.

Abrupt, harsh transitions, convulsive movements, the acute angles of the joints, limbs bifurcated like the branches of a tree create a sense of discord, dissonance, tumult, in fact, but all come together as a rhythmic whole, which moves on and on and never comes to rest. There are complexities of weight distribution, competing and opposed fields of force, violent shifts of direction, especially in the arm stretched in front of the chest like the trunk of an elephant (*gajahasta*).

In earlier times, in Mathura and thereafter, when the many-armed figures were first conceived, arms were placed on a single plane, which resulted in a static quality. In Shiva Dancing and finally in the Andhaka panel, the arms flail about in a disordered fashion, on different planes with angles created by bent elbows, though the overall movement is circular and clockwise. The arms are placed laterally as well as in perpendicular relationship to the background. In the classical mode, space and figure are not interdependent: mass exists separately, self-contained, and does not interfere with the negative environment around it. Many of the forms at Elephanta, piercing the surrounding space, extend beyond it and interrupt it haphazardly and chaotically by thrusts emerging out of the primary mass. This causes a sense of agitation or restlessness. But in the Shiva Dancing, as in all the other panels except the Andhaka, the face shows a trancelike expression that is in total contrast to the surrounding turbulence. Cosmic Shiva is divorced from his own activity in the world.

It should be pointed out that the Shiva Dancing panel, unlike the panels discussed above, has only one perfect view, which can be seen when one stands somewhat to the left of the nearest column. It is from here that separation from the background is seen to best advantage as the head and headdress (*makuta*) and the body in various angular thrusts are viewed in a three-quarter turn. The other views are flatter, and on Shiva's left the three-dimensional idea has not yet been worked out to perfection. An attempt at foreshortening fails in its purpose, resulting in a rather clumsy left side.

With centrifugal forces exploding, the figure of Shiva slaying the demon Andhaka is released from the background and propelled in a diagonal thrust out of a concave ground, as light from darkness, like the act of birth. Shiva's body is filled with energizing breath which presses out from within; an effect of great mobility and grandeur is achieved. Here as well, sudden turns of direction and extreme juxtaposition of contrasting forms create dissonance but not distortion. The three-dimensionality that was only tentatively grasped in the Shiva Dancing panel is here demonstrated with consummate finality. All the views are perfect. The sun itself appears *behind* the headdress as its rays, coming from the west, penetrate the excavated space.

Opposites are reflected in the narrative and in the visual style. All is contradiction, with reintegration as the goal. The modern visitor is not prepared; the opposites sometimes overwhelm, and often there seems to be no synthesis. But one can imagine that for the very gifted devotee, all becomes reconciled. A partial listing of polarities would include:

In the content of the narrative

1. Ravana presumes to bring chaos to the universe, but ultimately he is subdued and becomes a grateful penitent.

2. In the Gambling Scene panel the atmosphere of bliss on the mountain is temporarily interrupted when Shiva cheats at the game of dice. Shiva deserts

Parvati in anger and wanders about until Parvati, having transformed herself into a beautiful mountain maid, effects a reconciliation.

3. The Androgyne represents female and male energies united.

4. In Eternal Shiva, Aghora the fierce, male aspect (Pl.41), and Vamadeva, the feminine and charming aspect (Pl. 43), are united in Tatpurusha, symbolizing totality.

5. The force of the Ganges and Shiva's power are integrated in the headdress (Pl. 49) in the Ganges panel as the river floods down toward the earth, and Shiva raises himself to contain her force.

6. Shakti power and Shiva power are united in marriage in the Marriage panel.

7. The cycle of death and continual resurrection of the demon Andhaka (Pl. 60) by means of his drops of blood is brought to an end by Shiva's powers.

8. In the Shiva Dancing panel the dance of destruction brings about creation which again leads to destruction, and so on.

9. A seemingly weightless, transcendent Shiva is balanced on the stem of a lotus, symbol of the root pillar, which emerges from the chaotic turbulent waters in the Lord of Yogis panel.

In the style

1. Some figures merge with the parent rock and others are in the process of being propelled outward toward the space within the cave, which is an extension of the panel depths. In the Ganges panel Shiva is drawn into the rock, while his accompanying dwarf strides outward. Parvati of the same panel is held by the parent rock, her feet not really resting on the ground. There is a sense of disequilibrium, a Gothic sway, while in the Marriage panel, Parvati stands more firmly on the ground underfoot.

2. The frames press inward and toward the center, compressing the energies, while at the same time centrifugal forces press against the restraining frame. This is best studied in the Shiva Dancing. Eternal Shiva's upward ascension is awkwardly and abruptly contained by the ceiling of the chamber.

3. Transcendent, weightless figures like the guardian on the southeast corner of the shrine and Shiva with the Ganges contrast with the corporeally powerful, voluminous, solid mass, the blocklike figure of Shiva Lord of Yogis and especially the mighty and titanic Shiva in the Gambling Scene panel.

4. The figures of Shiva are less prone to the particularizing tendencies reserved for the less godly. In all the panels he is depicted in a style that is open—a single, solid volume, with plain and unadorned surfaces, undisturbed by mod-

eling, with avoidance of concavities. Appropriate spatial placement establishes his solidity, individuality, self-containment, and strength. But at the same time closely packed clusters of small forms which fragment the field and agitate it flank or overhang the major volumes. In the single figures, we observe elaborately and intricately carved headdresses placed above faces with transcendent, passionless, somnolent expressions.

5. Figures tend to move toward one another, while at the same time maintaining their independence from one another.

6. From the bottom corners of the composition in the Ravana panel, all the elements rise to a vertex; Shiva in the Andhaka panel plunges out and soars upward; or in another instance, described by George Michell, the Eternal Shiva rises from the earth. But the heavy blocklike bases pull the pillars down toward the earth, and the tyranny of the ceiling and some of the upper portions of the frames inhibit and limit ascension.

7. Emerging like a giant unfolding flower Eternal Shiva is also the unchangeable and straight root pillar; and the unfolding of the lotus capitals of the pillars, which close in upon themselves, evolve out of rigid bases (Pl. 19).

8. Linear time is expressed in episodes as in the Ganges and Andhaka panels; cyclical time is expressed in the dance of Shiva; eternal time is expressed in the middle face of Eternal Shiva, Tatpurusha (Pl. 43).

9. Cacophonic effects are contrasted to those that produce stillness.

10. Mobility and immobility are depicted at their most extreme states.

11. Closed patterns (for example, the Vishnu circle in the Androgyne panel) (Pl. 34) exist independently in contrast with transmutable, nonpatterned areas, which have a tendency to coalesce (as in the flying figures of the Ravana panel) (Pl. 71).

12. Some panels, like the Marriage, emphasize fluid outlines with rounded contours and with gradual transitions; others stress angular, sharp transitions. Entry into the cave initiates a process whereby contradictions are unmasked and then brought to resolution.

From one point of view everything in the cave exists only as a stimulus to the psyche to uncover what lies deep within the Self; thus everything depends upon the experience of the reacting person. While some medieval devotees had a firm grasp of the abstract concept of Shiva, then as now, for many, the divine was first and foremost manifested in less sublime but more familiar places. To reach these people, the artist made the Brahmanical symbols inseparable from the more elemental modes of worship. There does not seem to be any form of ancient worship that is not alluded to at Elephanta. The goddesses, lush vegetation, the moon, water, blood, fire, stone, mountain, and animals—snakes, bull, elephant, goat, horse, Garuda bird (Pls. 34, 48), lion, composite animal (*makara*)—all are portrayed in disciplined sensual abundance, uniting with nature's profusions on the island. Thus all who come to worship find sustenance here. Ishana, who is so high in the ladder of manifestation that he must not be concretely depicted, is there above the Eternal Shiva, implied. One who is capable of such a conception can be with god at Elephanta, but so can one who is reacting to more recognizable and intimate symbols, which to him are not symbols but god.

Although the sculpture is characterized by a luxurious proliferation of forms, the underlying conception is nevertheless ultimately reductionist and puritan in spirit.

Hundreds of years had already passed since the early Buddhist theology had provided the impetus for the excavation of monasteries and assembly halls, pure and pristine in their design. But by the fifth century, a change in style had taken place. At Aurangabad Cave 3 and Ajanta Caves 1 and 2, for example, the all too exuberant display of technically proficient ornamentation of the columns and other parts of the interior often bordered on excess of surface effects, reflecting the laxity of spirit which accompanied the Buddhist decline.

While retaining the complexities of organization of elements, the cave at Elephanta recaptures the earlier mode of restraint. The *linga* shrine perfectly expresses the rebirth of a severely austere style. Its walls are totally plain and bare, the doorways devoid of carving, the forms reduced to the purest geometric abstractions. Vast uncluttered space in the hall is punctuated at uniform intervals by columns which are made to resemble the most rudimentary vegetative forms. The figures of guardians and of Shiva and Parvati are depicted as virtually nude, needing no outer embellishment. A rebirth of religious spirit, seeking inviolable and primal connections with the deity, had inspired the creation of this inimitable monument which represented at the same time the culmination of a long tradition and also a new beginning.

GEORGE MICHELL

The Architecture of Elephanta: An Interpretation

THE CAVE TEMPLE on Elephanta island is the home of Shiva, the greatest of all the gods (Maheshvara-Eternal Shiva, Pls. 39, 40). It is the place where Shiva displays his paradoxical and mysterious nature in different forms. But the cave temple is much more than a setting for divine manifestations; it is an image of the heavenly mountain residence of Shiva and, on a higher level of association, of the structure of the universe itself. In fact, one of the chief characteristics of Shiva, his relentless energy, is identified with the cosmic rhythms of creation and destruction.

All the elements of the architecture at Elephanta are directed toward invoking the divine presence of Shiva and making visible notions about cosmic order. By a complex process of symbolism parts of the cave temple and, more significantly, ritual movements within the interior space are identified with Shiva and the universe that he controls. Not only is the mythology of the god illustrated in elaborate sculpture panels but the very layout of the cave temple—in terms of space, light, and movement—is itself a myth. Here the devotee leaves the world of man and progresses toward the world of the gods; the rituals he performs permit a communication between human and divine spheres.

Everything about Elephanta suggests a withdrawal from the everyday world. Several journeys have to be undertaken in order to reach the cave: water must be crossed, a mountain climbed, and a cave entered (Pls. 1, 2, 3). For the devotee this passage across, upward, and inside is interpreted as a progression toward the god. There is no outer elevation to the cave temple, only the natural mountain, the image of which always dominates the interior space of the cave within the mountain. Access is through three entrances on the east, north, and west sides, actually excavated trenches. On the east and west the entrances lead from artificially created sunken courtyards with minor shrines (not considered here).

The interior of the cave is clearly laid out (Pls. 18, 19), the space being divided into a number of aisles by columns. These columns have tapering shafts and

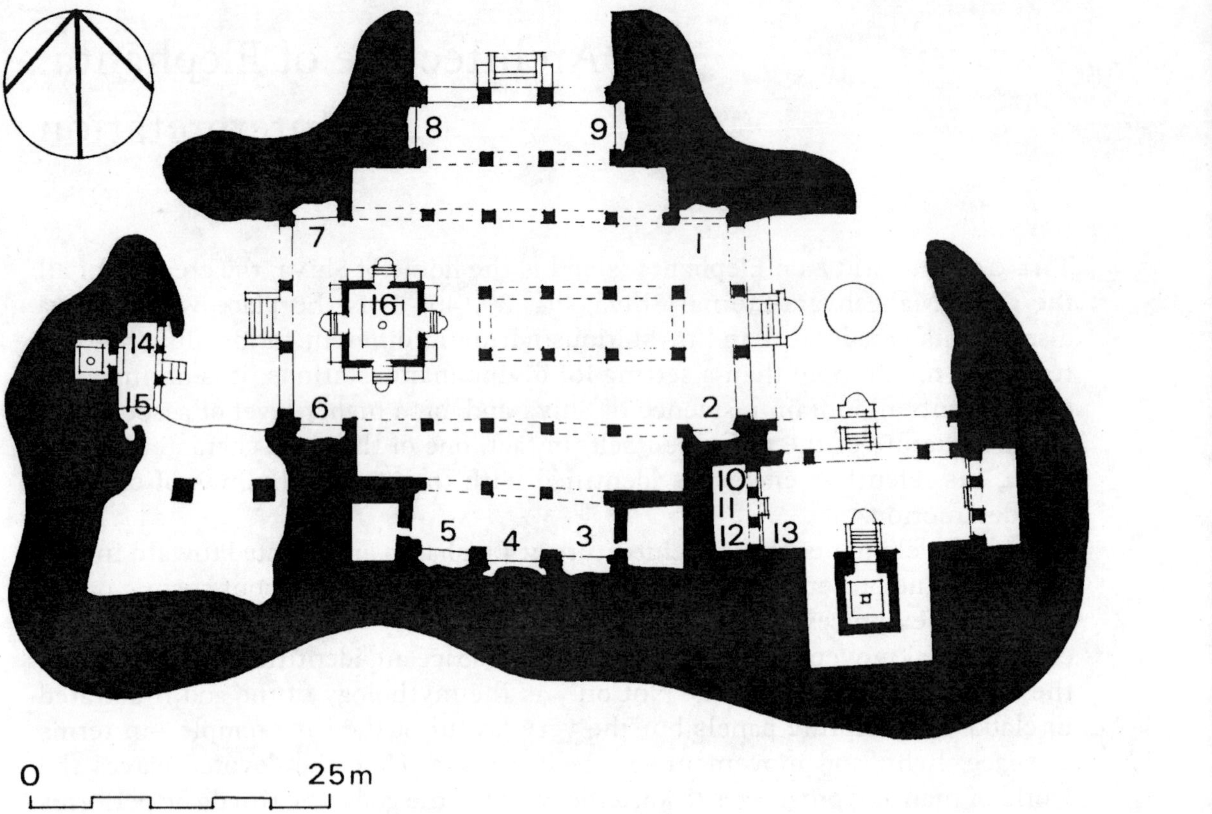

Fig. 1. Key to the sculptures at Elephanta.

Main Hall

1. Ravana
2. Gambling Scene
3. Androgyne
4. Eternal Shiva
5. Ganges
6. Marriage
7. Andhaka
8. Shiva Dancing
9. Lord of Yogis

East Wing Shrine

10. Karttikeya
11. Matrikas
12. Ganesha
13. Dvarapala

West Wing Shrine

14. Lord of Yogis
15. Shiva Dancing

Main Hall Shrine

16. Linga

FIG. 2. Plan of the main cave at Elephanta.

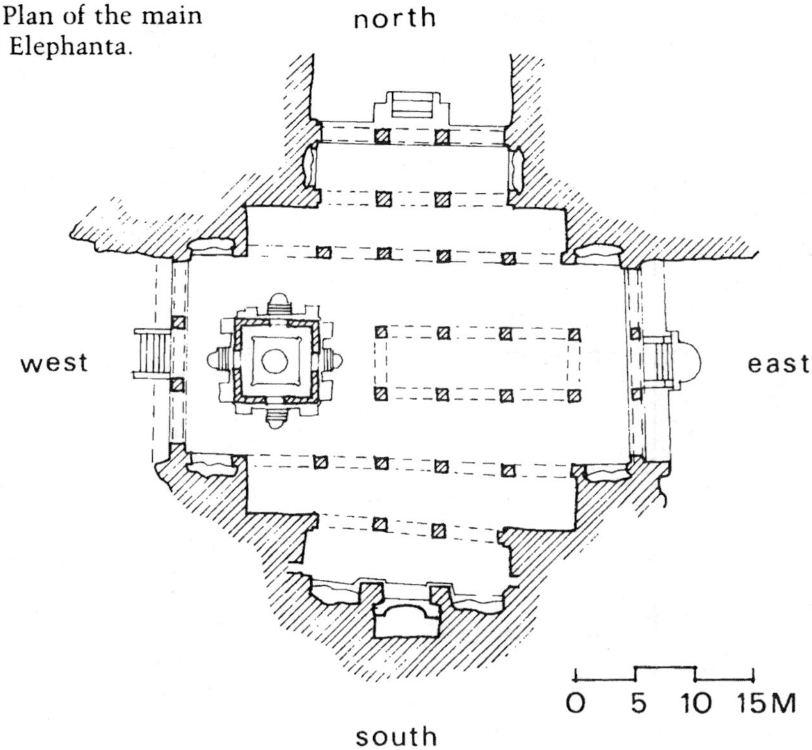

fluted, "compressed-cushion" capitals. Above the capitals are brackets supporting "beams" which run along the ceiling, articulating the space. There is a slight variation in height throughout. Inside this columned space, toward the west entrance, is a square sanctuary (Pls. 4, 5, 6) detached from the walls; inside this sanctuary is a monolithic *linga* (Pls. 7, 8). Sculpture panels deeply carved into the walls are positioned at either side of the three entrances and along the south wall. Other than the carved columns and wall panels the architecture of the interior is plain and massive (Figs. 1, 2).*

Of great significance is the symmetrical plan. Although excavated somewhat irregularly out of solid rock, it is not difficult to establish the original geometric concept of Elephanta. Two axes pass through the center of the space aligned with the cardinal points. Two concentric circles, their centers coinciding with the

* All figures in this essay are by the author.

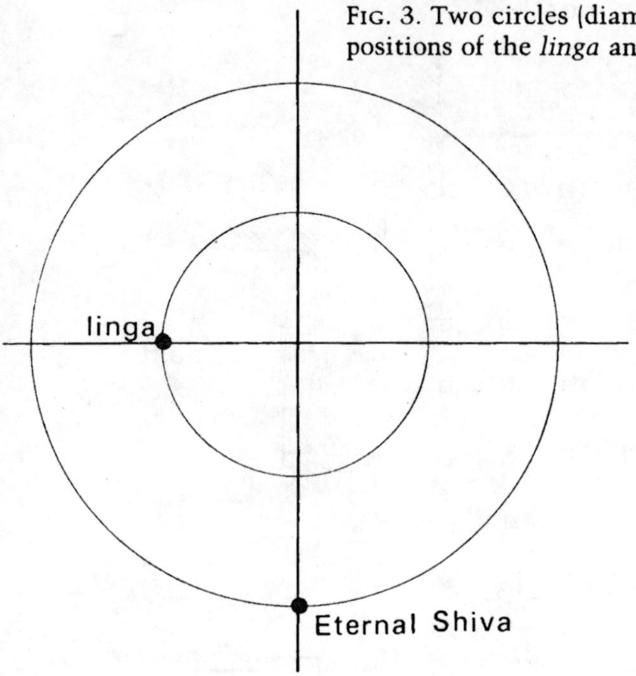

FIG. 3. Two circles (diameters in 1:2 proportion) determine positions of the *linga* and the Eternal Shiva image.

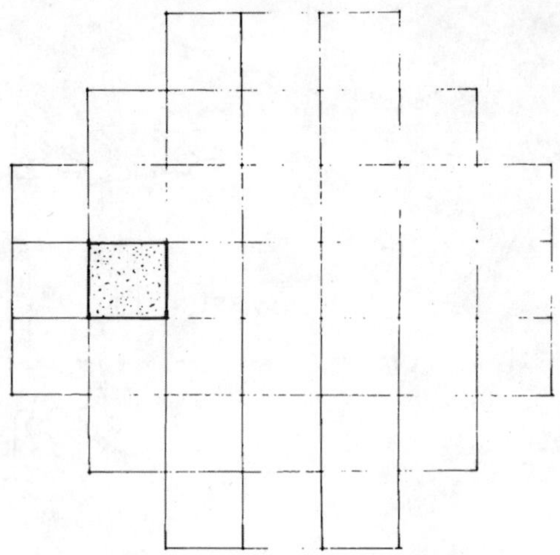

FIG. 4. Layout of the plan in squares. The dotted square indicates interior of the sanctuary. Thirty-six other squares create the columnal space.

intersection of these axes, determine the position of the *linga* in the center of the sanctuary on the east-west axis and the *furthermost* extensions of the plan—the three staircases at the east, north, and west entrances, and the Eternal Shiva image on the south wall (Fig. 3). (The three visible heads of this image, Pls. 39, 40, are deeply recessed into the wall, and there is the implication of a fourth unseen head. The circle and the north-south axis meet at a point coinciding with the center of the four heads, almost at the back wall of the niche.) In this way the two most important focal points within the cave—the *linga* and Eternal Shiva—are geometrically related. The two circles have diameters of about 22m and 44m (1:2). The columns creating the aisles, the sanctuary, and the stepped walls are laid out on squares, the corners of which coincide with the centers of the columns and along the walls (Fig. 4). Thirty-seven squares are symmetrically grouped in rows of 3, 5, and 7, running in both directions. One of these squares forms the interior of the sanctuary. Thus the number of squares creating the columned space is 36 (6 × 6), a number generally imbued with great significance

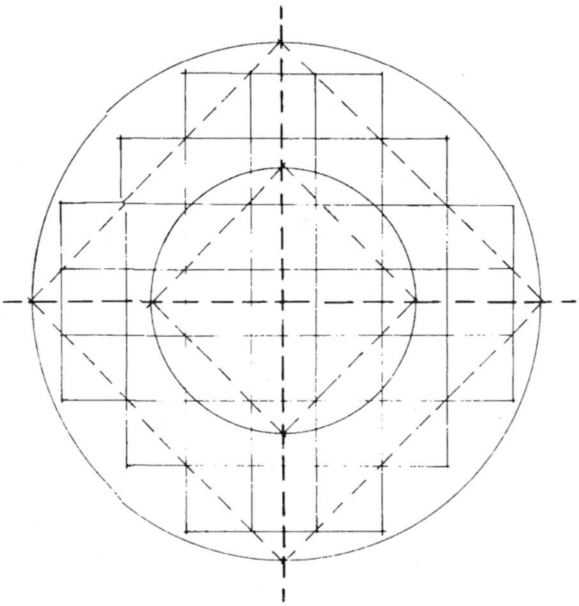

FIG. 5. Relationship of circles and squares.

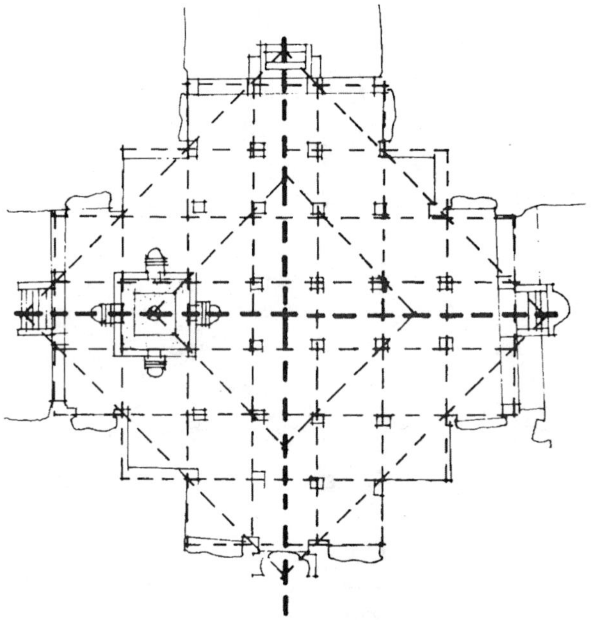

FIG. 6. Squares and axes superimposed on temple plan.

(as are other numbers in the series, 3 × 3, 4 × 4, 5 × 5, etc.). The squares are about 5.5m. (If this is taken as the basic unit for the plan, then the diameters of the circles are in the ratio of 4 × 5.5m and 8 × 5.5m.)

This fundamental geometry of the plan is actually a sacred mandala providing the interior space with a cosmic dimension through the medium of sacred mathematics. The circles are combined with the configuration of squares by means of diagonals passing through the squares (Fig. 5). Thus are related the center of the mandala, the position of the columns, walls, beams, and staircases, and also the two focal points of the interior—the *linga* and Eternal Shiva (both with guardian figures). Related to the location of these focal points are rituals of movement within the cave expressed as two axes leading to the *linga* and Eternal Shiva (Fig. 6). These axes are probably the most original feature of the architectural layout.

Running east to west and north to south, the axes pass through the center of the cave (Fig. 7). The east-to-west axis links the east entrance to the sanctuary.

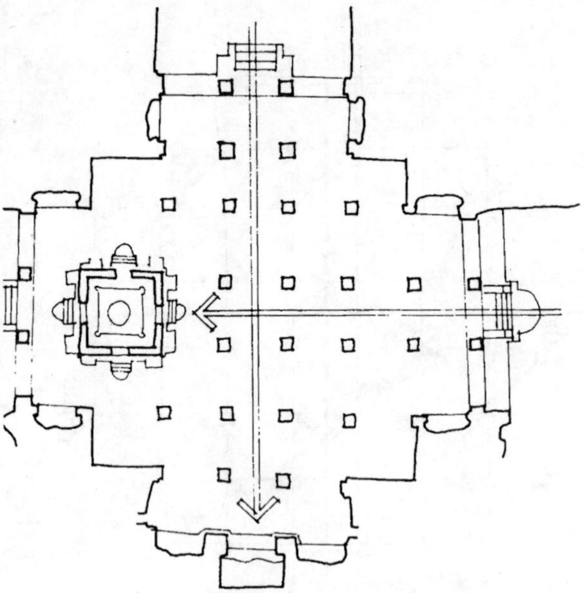

FIG. 7. East-to-west axis leads to the *linga*. North-to-south axis leads to Eternal Shiva.

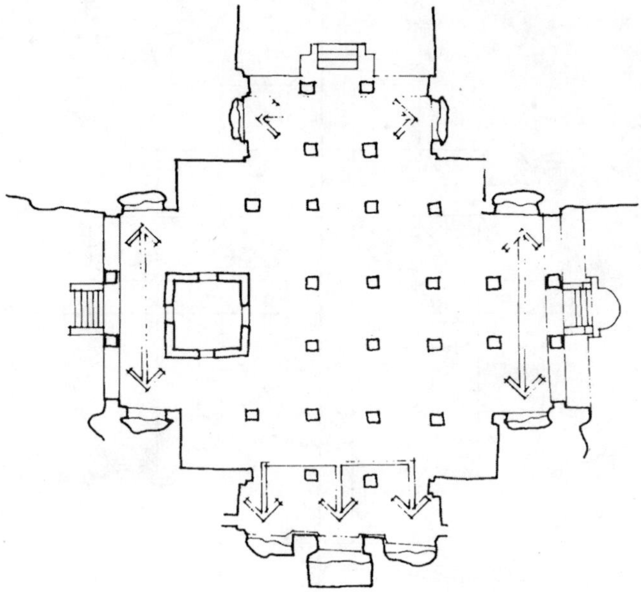

FIG. 8. Four groups of sculptures.

The "beams" connecting the column brackets mostly run in an east-west direction along the ceiling, creating a movement from the eastern entrance toward the sanctuary. Characteristic of this axis is the progression toward the *linga* at the center of the sanctuary, impressively silhouetted against the doorway behind, lit from the court beyond. The *linga* is the most significant point within the cave. It is housed in a sanctuary originally entered through four pairs of swinging doors flanked by colossal male guardian figures. They stand gracefully but powerfully posed, some with tilted hips, shoulders, and heads. Entering at the east end of Elephanta, then, the devotee progresses toward the *linga*. This is the direction toward a world beyond iconic forms.

Movement along the north-to-south axis is a different experience. Passing under the "beams" that traverse the interior space, the devotee penetrates deeper and deeper into the cave toward the great triple-faced Eternal Shiva. Leaving the daylight at the entrance, the devotee is increasingly enveloped in the surrounding darkness as he approaches Eternal Shiva. Movement along this axis is thus one of penetration from light to darkness, from outside to inside, always dominated by the stupendous triple-faced Shiva image.

Altogether, nine great sculpture panels are carved inside the Elephanta cave, forming a series describing the mysterious nature of the god to whom the cave is dedicated. Though their function is primarily one of didactic illustration, the sculpture panels also serve a secondary purpose as devotional icons. The panels are positioned within the interior space to create a carefully calculated "program" of related images.

The sculptures are divided into four groups—the panels facing each other at the north, east, and west entrances, and the trio of panels along the south wall (Fig. 8). The opening to the north, facing the sea and functioning today as the principal entry for innumerable tourists and pilgrims, is flanked by images of the Lord of Yogis (Pl. 68) (left) and Shiva Dancing (Pl. 64) (right). This is no accidental pairing, for these are the two most vividly contrasting images of Shiva ever to have been created by Indian artists. Here the energy of the god finds its most powerful and paradoxical expression: it is inward, silent, and still (as the yogi), also outward, noisy, and dynamic (as the dancer). Though presented as opposites, the energies of these two images of Shiva are actually identical; they are merely focused in different directions as a reminder of the fluid connection between outer and inner rhythms, of the unity underlying the different forms of the god.

At the east entrance and on the axis leading to the devotional focus of the cave are twin images of Shiva and Parvati seated on Kailasa, the celestial mountain residence of the god. These scenes, crowded with accessory figures, take place on the mythical world mountain, identified with the mountain in which the Elephanta cave is carved and inside which the devotee now penetrates. Great care has been taken by the artists of these panels to depict Shiva's mountain retreat, especially the rocky outcrops and flying divinities. Shiva and Parvati are here relaxed, for they are "at home": they gamble together (left), or Shiva casually suppresses Ravana, who had disturbed his peace (right).

Opposite, flanking the western entrance to the cave, are panels illustrating Shiva impaling Andhaka (left) and the marriage of Shiva and Parvati (right). As at the north entrance, these paired images illustrate opposing aspects of the god. The theme here, however, is contrast of mood rather than contrast of energy. Shiva is terrifying, active, and angry (as the destroyer of demons); also compassionate, calm, and happy (as the husband of Parvati). He is the god of the cremation grounds and of the inauspicious crossroads, in fact, of everything demonic; he is also the tender lover of the daughter of the mountain.

More complex associations are discovered in the three great panels on the south wall. To the left, Shiva and Parvati are joined in a single image (the Androgyne) (Pls. 31, 32) leaning against Nandi—the bull vehicle of Shiva and the embodiment of the procreative and agricultural nature of the god in animal form. To the right, Shiva assists in the descent of the river Ganges, which appears as a triple-bodied goddess (Pls. 44, 48, 49). Parvati looks on (Pl. 47). The Ganges is sometimes considered as Shiva's wife and the mother of Shiva's son, Skanda. These subtle male-female and husband-wife relationships are embodied in the enlarged three-headed image of Eternal Shiva, the great lord of the gods, the climax of all the sculpture panels. Here Shiva emerges from the mountain with only three of his four heads visible. (Implied is a fourth head, turned unseen into the mountain, and a body of the god, buried deep inside the mass of the rock.) The two side profiles express a feminine quality as well as a fierce and masculine aspect (right and left, respectively); the central full head is immobile, introspective, and serene—the male-female and active-passive dichotomies are here surpassed in what is perhaps the most powerful portrait of the god ever to have been fashioned in stone (Pls. 38-43). Positioned at the center of the south wall opposite the north entrance, this head faces directly out to sea, yet gazes deeply within.

Along the south wall, then, male and female aspects of Shiva express themselves in a number of complex iconographic forms, leading the devotee away from the limitations of the natural world into a sphere where opposites are subtly united. There is also a manipulation of human and animal forms, as in the Androgyne panel. Another motif is that of descent (illustrating the myth of the river Ganges) contrasting with the rising triple heads of the "submerged" Eternal Shiva.

Other less important relationships are also perceived in the distribution of carved panels. Four sculptures on the south wall depict Shiva with Parvati (in one instance united in a single image); the fifth and central image combines male and female aspects. Dynamic images of Shiva (as the dancer and destroyer) are reserved for the two panels at the northwest corners of the temple while to the northeast are peaceful images of the god (Lord of Yogis and the Ravana panel).

Let us return to the double axial system within the cave. No other example of Hindu sacred architecture presents this combination of ritual movements—one leading to the devotional focus, the other to an iconic focus. What meanings do these axes embody? What compelled the architects to invent such a scheme? The circumstances surrounding the excavation of this monument and the cults and rituals that once took place within it are now irrevocably lost to time. There is, in fact, an almost complete absence of any definite information about the historical, social, and religious context; it is not even clear in which century the

FIG. 9. Power of the *linga* radiates outward in four directions.

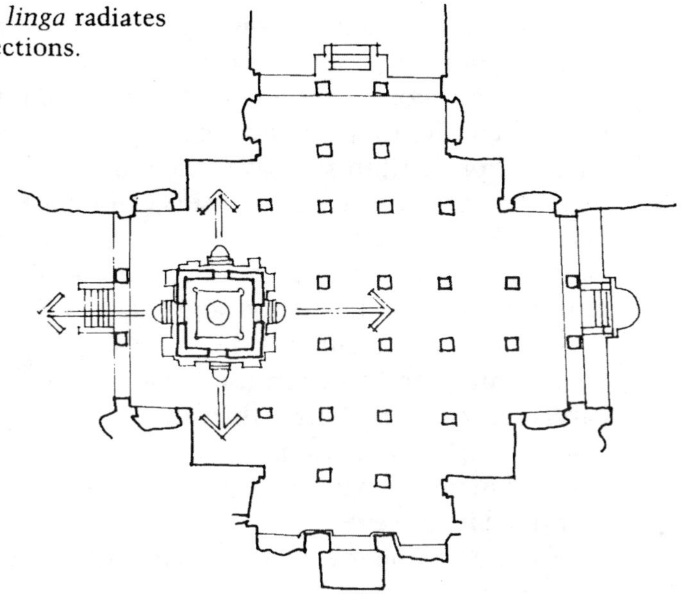

cave temple was excavated. Though interpretation can never replace history, some observations may be made.

The architecture of Elephanta clearly betrays an emphasis on duality. The east-to-west axis is that of devotion. It leads to the focus of worship, the *linga*, where the priest achieves direct contact with the god through well-prescribed rituals. As is usual in Hindu architecture, the direction of this movement is from east to west. This is the axis of prayer for priests and pilgrims. Outward, through doorways in four directions, radiates the power of the *linga*, benefiting visitors with an auspicious "looking on" (*darshana*) (Fig. 9). In contrast, progression southward has a distinctly theatrical effect, dominated always by the great triple-faced Eternal Shiva. This image is flanked by guardian figures with dwarf companions and by Shiva/Parvati scenes on either side. Here is the world of sacred icons, of the multitude of aspects and manifestations of Shiva. But how are these forms expressed, and what do they describe?

The grouping of the sculpture panels has already been discussed. Also of importance is their presentation. Walls and ceilings are undecorated; only the columns are carved. This was no oversight, for only in this way do the richly carved panels create their full visual impact. The panels are deeply carved and strongly framed, positioned well back from the walls in their own space. There, inside the wall frame, cosmic scenes take place. The forceful gestures and postures of the figures, the crowded compositions and the clearly mythical nature of the scenes truly express a celestial drama within a frame (proscenium). These are cosmic visions transporting the devotee into another world. The figures are larger than life; they fly or dance through the air; they sit on mountain peaks or emerge from within the cave; they are enclosed in an awe-inspiring silence or resonate with a heavenly music. Combined in celestial tableaux, the figures display their adoration of Shiva, acknowledging the god as the supreme principle of the universe. Despite these cosmic dimensions, the figures are undeniably human in form. In fact, Shiva and Parvati are the king and queen of the universe.

This "royal" quality of the sculpture is, perhaps, a significant clue to one of the meanings embodied in the layout of Elephanta. The great number of Shiva/Parvati images on the south wall has already been noted. Throughout Indian history kings have patronized Hindu temples and endowed them for repairs and maintenance. Though kings did not actually identify themselves with the gods enshrined in these temples, such monuments were sometimes named after their royal patrons. The involvement with the construction of temples and the rituals of worship that took place there, as well as the support of resident priests, was an effective method by which kings established political control and legitimacy of rule. In this manner the king ensured that his rule was divinely sanctioned and protected. In no other Hindu temple are the theatrical and royal qualities of the sculpture more obvious. This feature, in combination with the clearly demarcated double axial system, strongly suggests a division of devotional and other rituals. Perhaps at Elephanta there was an attempt to connect the royal patron of the cave and his queen (or queens), whoever they were, with the cosmic "royal family," Shiva and Parvati. In this way there may have been a desire to accommodate a royal ritual within the temple and the ceremonies associated with it, and to express this in terms of an axis of movement distinct from that for devotional use.

Whatever rituals actually took place within Elephanta when it was first completed, the monument remains one of the masterpieces of Hindu architecture and art. Even though there is a separation in time of much more than a millennium from the present century, Elephanta is still recognized as a powerful place. Visited each day by countless tourists who are more or less unfamiliar with fundamental notions of Shiva mythology and Hindu cosmology, the quality of the damaged sculptures and the clarity of the spatial layout never fail to impress. And then there are the fresh petals of brightly colored flowers placed early each morning on top of the *linga* and at the base of the great Eternal Shiva. The Elephanta is still alive, its cosmic reverberations still acknowledged.

WENDY DONIGER O'FLAHERTY

The Myths Depicted at Elephanta

ELEPHANTA IS THE HOME of Shiva. To be sure, he has other homes; he lives in numberless places across a long continuum of which the highest form is the special heaven of Shiva, beyond the reaches of the finite universe, and the smallest (though by no means the lowest) form is the place within the heart of every Shiva devotee (*bhakta*). Between these two extremes many sites can well claim to be the home of Shiva: Mount Kailasa in the Himalayas; Benares, sacred to Shaivas; Ellora, where another Kailasa is carved out of a single massive rock; and many shrines in South India that regard themselves—rightfully—as the center of the universe, the navel of the earth, the place most dear to God. Yet despite all of these valid claims, Elephanta is the place where the main events in the mythology of Shiva are depicted most powerfully, consistently, and exclusively. For other gods live at Benares, at Ellora, and in the Himalayas; small, local gods claim a share in the South Indian shrines. But at Elephanta there is nothing but Shiva. To spend a day at Elephanta is to spend a day outside of the world, or rather in another world: in *His* world.

To begin with, Elephanta is on an island; one reaches it by crossing quite a lot of water. This produces not only a feeling of isolation from the profane world but a special cosmological situation from the Hindu point of view: for India is an island (the "Rose-apple Island," Jambudvipa); and the world is an island, surrounded by concentric oceans of salt and milk and honey; and the universe is an island, a closed egg floating in the cosmic waters. Here, therefore, one is at the center of the center of the center; and these converging spheres are reinforced by the layout of every Hindu shrine, including this one.

The water makes it difficult to reach Elephanta; one cannot stumble upon it by accident. This, too, resonates with Hindu ideas about the house of god; for every temple is carefully guarded by strong, forbidding doorkeepers (Pls. 4, 5, 6, 12-15, 22-24). The mythology surrounding doorkeepers is at the heart of Shiva's world. These are the keepers of the threshold, literally and quintessentially "liminal" in Victor Turner's sense of the word: they symbolize the challenge of our passage from the profane world into sacred space, and this is always a difficult and dangerous transition. The corpus of myths about Shiva is rich in incidents where those who burst in upon the god without proper invitation come to grief; chief among these are the episodes of Kama, Agni, Adi, Ganesha, Parashurama, Bhrigu, Vishvaksena, Ila, and Ravana.

Kama. When Shiva was performing his asceticism (*tapas*) in solitude, the gods wished to have him marry and beget a child to defeat the demon Taraka. To this end, they sent the god of erotic love (Kama) to interrupt Shiva's meditation. Taking the form of a bee or a perfumed breeze to elude the servants of Shiva who had been stationed to guard him, Kama succeeded in breaking Shiva's trance—only to have Shiva open his third eye and burn Kama to ashes.

Agni. When Shiva did in fact marry, the gods waited eagerly for a child to be born; but Shiva had the uncanny ability to make love for several centuries without ceasing or letting his seed fall; this was due to his great yogic powers. Unable to wait any longer, the gods sent Agni, the god of fire, to interrupt Shiva in his loveplay. Agni took the form of a parrot to elude the doorkeepers and interrupted Shiva in bed with his wife Parvati. Furious, Shiva cursed Agni to take his (Shiva's) seed in his mouth and to become pregnant, a state which Agni found embarrassing, painful, and a serious problem.

Adi. On another occasion after the marriage, Shiva's wife went away for a while; to prevent Shiva from his notorious philandering, she stationed her son Viraka (Little Man) at the door to keep women from entering Shiva's room. The demon Adi was determined to kill Shiva; to do this, he decided to take advantage of Parvati's absence by assuming the form of a woman and killing Shiva by mutilating him through sexual contact. To elude Viraka, Adi took the form of a serpent; once inside, he became a woman and Shiva made love to him. But at the crucial moment, Shiva realized his error and killed the demon; and Parvati, thinking that Viraka had failed as a doorkeeper, cursed him to become a stone.

Ganesha (Pls. 67, 70). Parvati was annoyed by Shiva's habit of coming into her room at will, even when she was bathing. One day she created a child out of the dirt that she rubbed off her body during a bath; this child was Ganesha. She stationed him at the door to prevent Shiva from entering, but when Shiva came to see her and met with unexpected opposition, he fought with Ganesha and beheaded him; later, he replaced the head with that of an elephant.

Parashurama. Shiva then stationed Ganesha at *his* door to prevent anyone from disturbing him while he was asleep. One day Parashurama came to see Shiva and was furious at being denied access to the god. He attacked Ganesha and broke off one of his tusks, but Ganesha remained steadfast.

Bhrigu. In order to test the three great gods (Brahma, Vishnu, and Shiva) to see which was the greatest, Bhrigu visited each in turn. When he reached Shiva, he discovered that Shiva had stationed his doorkeeper, Nandi (a bull, or a bull-headed man), there to prevent interruptions while he made love to Parvati. Furious at this insult to a Brahmin, Bhrigu cursed Shiva to be worshiped as a *linga* (phallus) (Pl. 7), the object to which Shiva had been devoted when he should have been paying attention to his visitor.

Vishvaksena. Once Shiva beheaded Brahma and had to beg for alms, holding the skull of Brahma in his hands. He came to beg from Vishnu, but Vishnu's doorkeeper, Vishvaksena, would not let him in. Shiva beheaded Vishvaksena and then continued to wander, garlanded with the skull and bones of Vishnu's doorkeeper; this form of Shiva is known as Kankala.

Ila. One day when Shiva and Parvati were making love in the forest, a group of sages interrupted them. In anger, Parvati cast a spell upon the forest so that any male creature entering it would become female. Some time later, King Ila came there, riding on his stallion; immediately he became a woman, and the stallion became a mare.

Ravana (see below: Ravana lifting Kailasa) (Pl. 70).

From this cluster of myths, it is evident that the doorkeeper is in as much danger as the one who tries to cross the threshold, if not more. It is also evident that the two roles are closely related: Shiva is often protected by doorkeepers (in the episodes of Kama, Agni, Adi, Parashurama, Rama, and Bhrigu) or by a magic spell that serves as a doorkeeper (in the tale of Ila), but he also attacks them (in the episodes of Ganesha and Vishvaksena) when he himself wants to break down a barrier. Doorkeepers are also used both to prevent sexual contact (as in the episodes of Kama, Adi, Ganesha) or to preserve sexual contact (in the case of Agni, Bhrigu, and, by implication, Parashurama). Most of the doorkeepers are regarded as the sons of Shiva (Viraka, Ganesha, Nandi), though they may work against Shiva (as in the episodes of Adi and Ganesha) or for him (as in the episodes of Parashurama and Bhrigu).

Who are these doorkeepers, and what do they symbolize? As the devotee wishes to enter the presence of God, he may see the doorkeeper in the temple as a threat to him on the brink of the frightening but wonderful world of the god's private room. One cannot but note the sinister implications of the fact that the god *does not want to be interrupted*; the doorkeeper is stationed to keep people *out*. On the other hand, the doorkeeper is doomed to be physically mutilated and overcome; the god cannot have his privacy; the intrusion must take place. For the conquest of the doorkeeper represents the triumph of union, often expressed through sexual metaphors: Kama *does* excite Shiva's lust, though he pays for it; Agni *does* get Shiva to produce a child; Adi unites physically with Shiva, though it costs him his life; and the two devotees (Parashurama and Bhrigu) reach the god even when he prefers one union (with his consort) to another (with his devotees). Finally, when Shiva himself is standing at the door, either as a lover (of Parvati) or as a worshiper (of Vishnu), he cannot be kept out. Ultimately, therefore, the doorkeeper symbolizes danger to the worshiper about to enter the temple (a danger often represented by depicting the doorkeeper as a fierce lion or a mythical animal resembling a griffin) as well as the assurance that he will ultimately reach his god. Though the doorkeeper or interloper is often mutilated, he is restored: Kama, though disincarnate, is more powerful than ever; Agni has the boon of being omnivorous though never polluted; Viraka is released from his curse; Ganesha's elephant head gives him his strength and wisdom; Ila is given a special dispensation to be a man one month, a woman the next. Even the demons Adi and Ravana benefit from their threshold encounters with the god, for each dies a consecrated death: Adi in the *Liebestod* with the god whom he hates and loves, Ravana killed by Vishnu but saved by his devotion to Shiva. A final link between the crossing of thresholds and the danger of literally losing one's head is the image of the disembodied head or Kirttimukha (head of fame) that is placed above so many temple doorways. According to various traditions, this is the head that was cut off in a threshold battle—the head of Vishvaksena, or of Parashurama, or of Viraka. It is, in any case, the head of the doorkeeper who survives despite his mutilation—indeed, who becomes immortal because of it, remaining at his post to warn the would-be interloper of the risks and rewards in what he is about to undertake.

Secondary Figures

Two of the figures in the east wing shrine are sons of Shiva who are doorkeepers: Ganesha (Pl. 64) and Karttikeya (or Skanda) (Pls. 35, 67). They flank the central shrines as their stories flank his; they are outgrowths of him, literally and symbolically. The stories of their births have been briefly alluded to in the discussion of doorkeepers; some further details will be offered here.

Ganesha. There are several different myths about the birth of Ganesha and the cause of his beheading. In one, Parvati asks Shiva for a child but he refuses to give her one; she then makes a child out of a piece of her sari, but when Shiva sees how handsome the child is, and how Parvati gazes at his face, he glances at him, touches him with his hand, and the child's head falls to the ground. Shiva then sends Nandi to find a new head; after a long battle, Nandi takes the head of the royal elephant belonging to Indra, the king of the gods. With the elephant's head upon his shoulders the child comes back to life and is welcomed by all the gods, who bring him many gifts.

Another variant emphasizes Ganesha's ambivalent, liminal character as a doorkeeper. The gods complained to Shiva that by granting boons to demons who became his devotees he was making it impossible for the gods to conquer the demons; they asked him, therefore, to create obstacles for the demons. Shiva then created Ganesha as the Lord of Obstacles (Vighnesha), to create obstacles for evil people (like demons) and to remove obstacles in the way of good people (like gods). The elephant is well suited as a remover of obstacles, as is his vehicle, the rat, who can gnaw through any obstacles to reach food or find his way out of any maze. Ganesha is worshiped at the beginning of any undertaking and so is appropriately stationed near the periphery of the Elephanta complex.

In a recent paper abstracted from his forthcoming major book about Ganesha, Paul Courtright has advanced a useful hypothesis that is highly relevant to the present discussion. He suggests that the myth of Ganesha's creation by his mother and painful sundering from her, and his restoration by his father, represents the enactment of the ritual of initiation, in which the child leaves his mother and, after a painful initial confrontation, becomes reconciled with his father or guru. This further combines the theme of familial conflict with Ganesha's role as god of undertakings, of which initiation is the archetype. One might further suggest that the head which is "replaced" upon Ganesha's neck is in fact his true head, unknown to him until he receives it in the initiation ceremony (as many initiates first receive their true name), just as Dadhyanch receives the horse-head that is truly his own only after he has entered into a sacrificial agreement with the gods.

Ganesha's key role as god of doorways and of beginnings, and his position at Elephanta at the east wing, lends support (though by no means definitive support) to the argument that one is intended to enter Elephanta through the east.

Skanda (Karttikeya). Skanda is the son of Shiva born because of two incidents described above. As a result of Kama's attack, Shiva married Parvati; and as a result of Agni's interruption, Shiva's seed was given to the gods. The seed made Agni pregnant (a condition that he transmitted to the rest of the gods, as he transmits all offerings made into him) but being unable to bear the burning seed he placed it in the Ganges. She, too, was unable to bear it and cast it up on her shore in a clump of reeds. The six Pleiades (Krittikas) were bathing in the Ganges and became impregnated by the seed (or, in other versions, found the child in the clump of reeds). They nursed him, and in order to suckle from all at once the child sprouted six heads. As soon as Skanda was born, Parvati's breasts began to stream with milk, and she knew she had had a son (albeit at a far remove); the Ganges also claimed him as hers, and so he is known as Gangeya (son of Ganges); and since the Krittikas mothered him, he is known as Karttikeya (son of the Krittikas). So too, both Agni and Shiva are his fathers. The multiple parentage of Skanda is in part the result of the conflation of several myths and cults but also an expression of his complex nature; furthermore, as Skanda is a hero—the general of the army of the gods—one may see in his birth the familiar pattern of the birth of the hero, born in a clump of reeds (or bullrushes, probably phallic images) or floating in a box on the river (probably an image of the womb), whose true parents are royal and/or divine in contrast with his lowly foster parents. These patterns may be seen in the myths surrounding Moses, Jesus, Krishna, Oedipus, and many other heroes; parallels with the story of Oedipus may also be seen in the conflict between Ganesha and Shiva.

The two sons often compete for the approval of their parents, in traditional sibling rivalry. Skanda is the athlete of the pair, a soldier but not a heavy thinker. Pot-bellied Ganesha, with his love of sweets, is the intellectual; as patron deity of scribes, he is invoked at the start of every manuscript. In keeping with these characteristics, Ganesha usually outsmarts his brawnier brother: once when Skanda challenged him to a race around the world, Ganesha simply waddled around his two parents (who are the mother and father of the world) and won the wager. Skanda is said to be married to Army of the Gods incarnate as a goddess (as well as to several other local goddesses in South India, where his cult probably originated); Ganesha is sometimes said to be a bachelor, like his father, and sometimes said to be married to Success and Intelligence incarnate (Siddhi and Buddhi).

The Eight Mothers (Matrikas). These goddesses are obscure and multilayered members of the Hindu pantheon. On the classical or "Sanskrit" level, they may be identified with the Pleiades or Krittikas, the mothers of Skanda; this explains their presence next to Skanda and Ganesha in the east wing at Elephanta. But they have another, darker, side as well; as servants of the orgiastic, murderous goddess Kali they are killers and drinkers of blood, in contrast with their roles as givers of milk in the "high" tradition. In their badly mutilated state at Elephanta it is hard to say which aspect prevails, but one would be inclined to look for both at once.

The Main Panels

The central image in the west wing shrine, Yogishvara, also appears as one of the main panels and will be discussed in its major form. Of the central panels, five depict Shiva with Parvati and four depict him alone.

SHIVA AND PARVATI

The Marriage of Shiva and Parvati (Kalyanasundara) (Pl. 51). Parvati, the daughter of the mountain Himalaya, fell in love with Shiva and wanted to marry him, but Shiva had vowed eternal chastity. When the attack of Kama failed to get immediate results (though Shiva was noticeably shaken from his yoga), Parvati devoted herself to severe asceticism to win the god. Shiva came to her in disguise as an old Brahmin and wondered aloud why such a voluptuous young girl (with a substantial dowery, to boot) should want to marry a renegade, penniless, disgusting ascetic like Shiva. When Parvati became furious and rose to the defense of Shiva, the old Brahmin revealed his true form and asked her to marry him then and there. "But," said Parvati, "you must ask my father for my hand." Impatient though he was, Shiva realized that even God must honor human conventions—which are natural and cosmic in their implications. So the formalities were honored, and Shiva came to marry Parvati. Vishnu gave the bride away, and is depicted at Elephanta to the left of Shiva; Himalaya, who consented to the match, is behind Parvati. Brahma acted as the priest, kneeling before them to offer the oblation into the fire; and all the gods came to witness the ceremony. Some texts state that during the ceremony Brahma caught a glimpse of Parvati's face and was so intoxicated by her beauty that he spilled his seed upon the ground and tried to cover it up with his feet. Shiva's yogic vision spied him out, however, and Shiva was about to attack Brahma when Vishnu interceded to remind them of their identity as two aspects of God, and the wedding proceeded without further incident.

Shiva Holding the Ganges (Gangadharamurti) (Pl. 44). The marriage, however, was certainly not without further incident. One day King Sagara's sixty thousand sons were burnt to ashes by an angry sage; the king's grandson Bhagiratha propitiated the Milky Way (Pl. 49) in heaven and begged her to descend to earth to revive the dead princes. She agreed to do this only on condition that someone would be able to break her fall from such a great height, or else she would shatter the earth. Shiva agreed to do this: he stood in the Himalayas and the river (called the Ganges on earth) cascaded onto his head, wound slowly through his thick, matted locks, and finally came to earth and revived the sons.

But since the Ganges is (like all Indian rivers) female, she is regarded as the wife of Shiva; we have already seen that she is a mother of Shiva's son, Skanda. Parvati therefore regards this act of cosmic soteriology as simple, bare-faced adultery. In the panel at Elephanta, one may see a forced quality in her pose (the textbooks say that she should look "uneasy") as Shiva receives the Ganges on his head. Everyone else, however, is full of joy: the Ganges herself (three-headed, as she is said to have three streams in heaven or to be joined by the Sarasvati and Yamuna rivers on earth), the sage Bhagiratha (kneeling directly on Shiva's left), the deformed servants (*ganas*) of Shiva who cluster around Parvati, and the gods who swarm about their heads (Pl. 44).

Ravana Lifting Kailasa (Pl. 70). Ravana was the demon king of Lanka (later famed as the abductor of Sita, wife of Rama). One day as he was traveling in the mountains, he came to the clump of reeds where Skanda had been born; there, his chariot refused to move. Nandi told him that Shiva and Parvati were making love on the mountain (Kailasa) and that this had stopped his chariot at the boundary. Unable to brook this insult, Ravana lifted Kailasa up by its roots, frightening Parvati, but Shiva pressed the mountain down with his toe, pinning Ravana under it. As Ravana continued to roar and flail in impotent rage, Shiva reassured Parvati. Eventually, Ravana praised Shiva for a thousand years, and Shiva forgave him and released him to return to Lanka. This myth (which is yet another variant of the theme of crossing dangerous thresholds) is depicted in a sadly mutilated panel at Elephanta; though Parvati has no head, she clings to Shiva, and he leans toward her to calm her, while Ravana whirls about beneath them, helpless.

Shiva and Parvati Gambling at Dice (also called Umamaheshvara and Parvati in Pet) (Pl. 26). The marriage of Shiva and Parvati is plagued by quarrels, often inspired by Shiva's persistent adulteries or by his yogic aloofness from domestic life. These grievances often erupt when the couple are playing dice, an act of cosmic significance: the four throws of the dice are the four ages of the world (Yugas), and to say that God plays dice is to state (*pace* Albert Einstein) that our fate is the result of a combination of accident and the whims of the gods. When Shiva and Parvati play dice, surrounded by their servants and by the hosts of the gods, Shiva always wins—by cheating, as often as not. When Parvati points this out, an argument ensues in which Shiva pulls rank: he blots out all the stars, or extinguishes the sun and moon, or indulges in some similar act of cosmic hooliganism, until Parvati tactfully withdraws her accusation.

Shiva as the Androgyne (half-man, half-woman—Ardhanarishvara) (Pl. 31). When the world began, Brahma, the creator, tried to produce living creatures, but they failed to reproduce themselves, since he had neglected to create women. Unable to extricate himself from this dilemma, Brahma asked Shiva to help him; Shiva took the form of an androgyne, making the left side of his body into a woman; the two parts separated, merged in sexual union, and produced all living creatures. This is the ancient image of the androgyne that must split in order to be creative. Later mythology says that Parvati, who was a separate being, married Shiva and then became half of his body for any of several different reasons: 1)

Shiva once embraced her so closely, in gratitude for her having fed him when he failed to get any food by begging, that their bodies merged into one. 2) The sage Bhringin had taken a vow to walk around only Shiva in worship, refusing to honor Parvati; to thwart him, Parvati persuaded Shiva to let their bodies merge into the androgynous form (a device that failed to stop Bhringin, who took the form of an insect and bored a hole through the middle of the couple, thus circumambulating Shiva alone). 3) In order to prevent Shiva from carrying on with other women, Parvati made him join his body with hers.

Although the androgyne is a symbol of perfect union, it can also prove barren (for in the earlier myth the two halves must separate in order to procreate) or antierotic (for the fused couple cannot *unite* when they are already *together*). In its highest form, however, it represents the ideal of the union of opposites (*coincidentia oppositorum*), the union of the worshiper and the god with whom he is in fact consubstantial, the simultaneous experience of longing and union, desire and satiation. Parvati on the left holds the mirror that symbolizes the woman's role in reflecting the man, as the moon reflects the sun; Shiva on the right is accompanied by his bull Nandi and worshiped by the gods, including the four-headed Brahma. Both have four arms, and the image is exquisitely balanced and blended. This is an androgyne that is neither splitting nor fusing; it is a statement of an eternal process caught in its essential moment of truth.

Shiva Alone

Shiva Impaling the Demon Andhaka on his Trident (Andhakasuravadha) (Pl. 59). One day, Parvati playfully covered Shiva's eyes with her hands, and darkness covered the universe; but a drop of sweat came out of Shiva's brow and was heated in the third eye in the middle of his forehead. It became an angry child named Andhaka, born of Shiva and Parvati. He was adopted by the demon Hiranyanetra (Golden Eyes) and grew up in the underworld. Years later, he fell in love with Parvati and wished to carry her off, but Shiva took Andhaka up, placed him on the tip of his trident, and began to dance. Andhaka's sins and flesh were burnt away by Shiva's fiery gaze, and he praised Shiva; then Shiva took him home, and Parvati accepted him as her own son. Shiva made him one of the leaders of his troops and gave him the name of Bhringin. Andhaka's blood was drained from his body (caught in the cup in Shiva's hand), and so Bhringin is a mere skeleton.

The Oedipal content of this myth is blatant. To the Hindu, however, the more important point is that Andhaka is transfigured and released by the violent action of the god. Thus the terrifying fangs and the swarm of arms carrying deadly weapons have an ultimately gracious effect: the god blesses those whom he destroys; death can be a passage to the supreme peace that is found only in the lap of the gods.

Lord of the Dance (Nataraja or Lalita) (Pl. 64). Shiva's dance takes two forms: the gentle erotic dance (*lasya*) associated with the creation of the world, and the violent, dangerous dance (*tandava*) associated with the destruction of the world. Both are said to have originated in the Pine Forest (Daruvana or Taraga), but the North and South Indian variants of the myth are significantly different. According to the former, a group of sages were living in the forest with their wives; to demonstrate to them that they had not yet subdued their lust and anger, Shiva came to the forest in the form of a handsome beggar, stark naked and with an erect phallus. He danced with the sages' wives and excited them; blind with rage, the sages cursed Shiva to be castrated. Like a bolt of lightning, his phallus fell to the ground, plunging the universe into darkness. The sages then realized who he was, and what they had done, and begged him to forgive them. He did so on condition that they worship his phallus (*linga*) forever. This myth appears only in relatively late Sanskrit texts and is the source of still later classical traditions that regard Shiva's dance as an act of cosmic creation. In South India, however, the castration is omitted from the myth; here it is said that when Shiva danced with the sages' wives, the sages hurled various weapons at him, which Shiva continued to dance into submission: they sent a tiger at him, but he flayed it and wrapped it around his shoulders like a shawl, and continued to dance; they conjured up fire against him, but he made it into a halo, and continued to dance; they sent a demon against him, but he trampled it under his feet, and danced on. This is the other dance, the destructive *tandava*, developing out of the thwarted erotic dance at the beginning of the myth. Clearly the two are closely related in the myth; so, too, the two dances of Shiva are merely two aspects of a single dance, for he destroys in order to create, tearing down in order to build up again.

The Lord of Yogis (Yogishvara, Mahayogishvara, or Lakulishvara) (Pls. 15, 68). This image, that appears in the west wing shrine as well as in a panel of the central shrine, is Shiva in his ascetic aspect. From his earliest appearance in Indian texts, Shiva has been associated with esoteric, meditative religions as well as with the sacrificial religion that Vishnu participates in. Shiva is a solitary god who withdraws into his mountain fastness on Kailasa for countless years until the gods must interrupt his trance—crossing his threshold—to beg his help in their business of keeping the world going. But Shiva's trance is not opposed to their creative activity; on the contrary, by meditating he stores up and enhances all those powers that make it possible for him to kill demons, beget heroes, and dance the world alive.

The image of the Lord of Yogis represents both this cosmic power and the ideal form of the human yogi. In particular, the yogi with a club may represent Lakulisha or Lakulishvara, the Lord with a Club, the founder of a Shaivite sect that was active at the time that Elephanta was carved.

The Eternal Shiva (Mahadeva, Maheshvara, Maheshamurti) (Pl. 39). This is by far the most commanding of all the images at Elephanta, by virtue of its placement, its enormous size, and its three-dimensionality (in contrast with the comparatively low-relief friezes on the surrounding panels). It is highly enigmatic and has inspired much conflicting interpretation, of which Stella Kramrisch's elaborate gloss of the "five-faced Shiva" is by far the most profound as well as the most convincing. But when viewed in the cave complex as a whole, its meaning can best be fathomed by looking at its placement and structure, for it presents the undifferentiated, unqualified, latent aspect of god (*nirguna*) in contrast with all the other specific, inflected, personified forms (*saguna*). If one also takes into account George Michell's hypothesis of the double focus of Elephanta, this colossal image may be seen as a still relatively "quality-possessing" (*saguna*) vision of the god, the doorway to the final and even less-inflected form, the *linga*.

The image of the Eternal Shiva can best be understood in the context of the overarching structure of Elephanta. Elephanta is a series of concentric circles, each less worldly and less detailed than the preceding. On the outermost periphery, the atmosphere of worldliness is expressed by commercialization and tourism rampant in the stalls that line the ascending staircase: postcards and mass-produced images, some of them depicting the images at Elephanta, some not. In the ancient days, when Elephanta was designed as a place of worship, only holy things would have been sold here, as they are still sold in the temple markets of South India: great piles of vermilion powders and rows of shining brass pots, brilliant flowers and books relating the origin and sanctity of the shrine. The temple market is the borderline of the two worlds, for what is being sold (among all the trinkets and modern overlays) is sacred stuff: food for gods (*prasada*) and vessels for holy water. The tawdry and shabby accretions of tourism in present-day Elephanta are a pale echo of what was once a highly charged threshold of the sacred and the profane, now entirely profane and thus providing a more violent and heady plunge into the sacred.

Past this threshold we enter the side shrines and then the main shrines, where we are overwhelmed by baroque detail; we have moved a little farther into the center, and the theological strip-tease is beginning to take place, for now all the detail is God's detail, not man's. The stones leap out at us and speak to us of the killing of demons and the marriage of goddesses, of domestic squabbles and cosmic dances, of yogic meditation and androgynous ecstasy. One's head begins to spin, the mind boggles, the eye cannot absorb it all.

Finally, surfeited by these incredibly detailed visions of the divine, one flees gratefully to the still center of the temple, the *garbha-griha*, the innermost shrine, the *sanctum sanctorum*—and here one encounters the god without specific attributes, the *nirguna* deity, the philosophical nexus of god. For whatever else the Maheshvara image may mean (and many scholars have gone to great lengths to explain it), it is certainly most striking in its simplicity and comparative lack of detail; here is a god who has gathered all his action into himself and remains completely latent, potential; one cannot tell what he is thinking, what he is about to do, or indeed if he has ever done anything or ever will; he is a complete enigma to us. His three faces are not without emotion, though it is hard to describe those emotions in words (and they change as the light changes, and as one's angle of vision changes; the massive head is a magnet for one's own projection onto the image); the faces are sensuous, joyful, threatening, peaceful, sad—so many things. And it is also possible to read much philosophical symbolism into the trinity of forms: time past, present, and future; creative, destructive, and sustaining aspects; and so forth. But one is ultimately left with the feeling that any statement at all will be inadequate, that this is the ineffable state of god in his totality, gathering into himself all the myriad of forms and functions that are depicted in the surrounding panels, and others that could have been depicted but were not, and others that never could be depicted at all.

The phallus (linga) (Pls. 8, 18). The Eternal Shiva image is spatially located where more conventional temples usually place the simplest image of all: the brutally bare and stark phallus of Shiva. This stone is literally a "sign" of the god, in a form even less differentiated than that of the Maheshvara. At Elephanta, the *linga* appears in a shrine all its own, surrounded by its own *dvarapalas*; it is a shrine within the shrine. Symbolically, though not structurally, this is the center of the temple complex. And although one has moved from a large physical space (the island as a whole, and then the outer boundary of the cave complex) to a small physical space (the small cave, cool and dark), the feeling is that one has been moving *outward* all the time, spiritually, into larger and larger spaces, until one encounters in the still center the simple image that is the totality of the universe. (Similarly, at the end of the Narnia books C. S. Lewis describes the end of the world and the entry of the elect into a tiny stable, in which there is a larger garden, in which there is a larger mountain, and so on, until the Faun explains, "The farther up and the farther in you go, the bigger everything gets. The inside is larger than the outside.") This is the heart of the god, an image whose simplicity can only be understood after one has seen its detailed manifestations in the living stones from all the other panels that capture, like still frames frozen out of the eternal stream of images, the activity of the god Shiva in the world.

The rich detail of the panels surrounding the *linga* and the image of Eternal Shiva is the whirling storm of Vedic religion, capturing the motion, eclecticism, and multifaceted flux that the worldly aspect of Hinduism celebrates. But wherever you are in the cave, you see out of the corner of your eye the still center represented by these two forms, the eyes of the storm, the promise of the Vedantic peace that remains a constant unattained ideal, an ideal that makes it possible to go on living in the cyclone. This peace is a very active one. The *linga* is not merely a centripetal force that draws the worshiper to the center; it is (like its human counterpart) something that partakes of expansion as its very nature, a centrifugal power constantly pushing outward. This quality of expanding form (which Coomaraswamy pointed out long ago as a basic quality of Indian art) finds its expression in the myth of the *linga* that grows infinitely great before the very eyes of Vishnu and Brahma. The calm of the *linga*, like the calm of the Lord of Yogis or the calm of Shiva pressing down on the turbulent Ravana, is symbolic of the constant tension between the desire for life and the desire for death, the tension of the super-ego pitted against the indefatigable id. The peace at the heart of Elephanta is a peace hard won, and a peace therefore all the more precious.

Bibliography

THE FOLLOWING major references serve as excellent introduction for the study of early Elephanta monographs.

1785 Gough, R., *A Comparative View of the Ancient Monuments of India, Particularly those in the Island of Salset near Bombay*, London, 1785.

Gough was the first to reprint accounts written by foreign visitors, who, with the coming of the Portuguese, began to take notice of the cave. Included are Linschoten, Ovington, Fryer, and Grose.

1871 Burgess, James, *The Rock-Temples of Elephanta or Gharapuri*, Bombay, 1871.

This is by far the best guidebook yet written. Serious attention is directed to architectural and iconographical details, to Sanskrit literature and Hindu concepts. There is also a comprehensive list of early accounts.

1882 *Gazateer of the Bombay Presidency*, vol. XIV, 1882, "Places of interest," p. 59.

This account leans heavily on Burgess' material. There is also a list of former writers, with a few variations.

1934 Sastri, Hirananda, *A Guide to Elephanta*, New Delhi, 1934.

This explains the topography, has a brief history and a description of the panels with measurements of the cave and a list of former accounts. (Reprinted, with commentary, by Ratan Parimoo, 1979.)

1977 Mitter, Partha, *Much Maligned Monsters: A History of European Reactions to Indian Art*, Oxford University Press, 1977.

Mitter analyzes most previous accounts in a masterful piece of research. The Elephanta material is dispersed in chronological order among the other accounts. The reader who wishes to study these early documents is well advised to read this book first.

Sixteenth-Century Accounts

1534 Da Orta, Garcia, *Coloquios dos simples e drogas . . . da India*, Goa, 1563. Translated by Sir C. Markham, *Colloquies on the Simples and Drugs of India*, London, 1913, pp. 444 ff.

Da Orta, a Portuguese botanist, was the first European to record his visit.

1538 De Castro, Joao, *Primeiro Roteiro da Costa da India desde Goa ate Dio* (Segundo MS. autographo) ed. Dioge Kopke, 1843, pp. 65-81. Reprinted in Mitter, p. 326.

A military hero, later Viceroy of Goa, De Castro was astounded by Elephanta.

He describes spatial relationships and some of the panels and is the first to measure an Indian monument.

1585 Van Linschoten, John Huyghen, *Itinerario*, Amsterdam, 1596. Ed. A. C. Burnell and P. A. Tiele, *The Voyage of John Huyghen Van Linschoten to the East Indies*, London, 1885, vol. I, 291.

Linschoten interprets the monuments as portraying monstrous images but nevertheless admires the workmanship. He identifies the island as Pory.

Seventeenth-Century Accounts

1616 Coutto, Diego De, *Of the very Remarkable and Stupendous Pagoda of Elephanta*, Decade VII, Book III, Chapter xi (1616), Communicated by the Rev'd V. K. Fletcher, *The Journal of the Bombay Branch of the Royal Asiatic Society*, vol. I, July 1841-July 1844, reprint, Byculla, 1870.

Although not accurately or always recognizably, Coutto gives a detailed description of the chapels and shrines with their measurements. He reports that lime covered the surface of the interior, that an inscription was sent to Portugal, and that "millions" of workmen were employed in the construction. He had no knowledge of Hindu iconography.

1689 Ovington, J. A., *A Voyage to Suratt in the Year 1689*, London, 1696, p. 158.

Ovington gives the dimensions and the count of pillars. He assumes the figures represented gigantic forms of the first race of mortals.

1698 Fryer, Johannes, *A New Account of East India and Persia*, London, 1698, pp. 73-74.

Dr. Fryer notices that the space is a square; he describes the elephant with a young one on its back and the carved horse. He describes the figures as giants and blames the Portuguese for the defacement.

Eighteenth-Century Accounts

1712 Pyke, Captain, "Account of a Curious Pagoda near Bombay," *Archaeologia*, vol. VII, London, 1785, 323; presented to the Society on February 10, 1780, by Alexander Dalrymple.

This is a valuable account of Pyke's visit in 1712, which he later recorded aboard ship. Plates show the elephant with a small one on its back, the horse, probably the first ground plan which recorded the fact that the cave approximated a square, and the likeness of a pillar. He makes assumptions about the panels, naming the Andhakasura as Solomon, etc. He considers the possibility of Chinese, Egyptian, or Alexandrian origin. He quotes from Fryer, Hamilton, Linschoten, and Ovington.

1727 Hamilton, Cap't A., *A New Account of the East Indies*, London, 1727, vol. I, 238-239.

This visitor was interrupted in his researches by a serpent that "made us take to our heels," and therefore there are few details.

1750 Grose, —, *A Voyage to the East Indies*, 1772, London, vol. I, 59-64.
Grose makes a plea for more scholarly attention and offers very generalized descriptions. He notices painting "round the cornishes," and "the beauty and freshness of the coloring."

1757 Ives, —, *Voyage from England to India in 1754*, London, 1773, p. 45.
Ives presents another ground plan, but the descriptions are inaccurate.

1760 Anquetil du Perron, M., *Zend-Avesta, Ouvrage de Zoroastre*, vol. I, Paris, 1771. Plate IV, opp. p. 394 and pp. 419-423.
Du Perron describes some of the panels and their measurements, but although he was interested in Hindu literature, he did not identify the iconography. He presents a ground plan.

1764 Niebuhr, C., *Voyages en Arabia en d'autre pays circonvoisins*, vol. II, Amsterdam, 1764, 25-33.
This volume marks a great step. Although Niebuhr's engravings, which he made from memory, are far from accurate, they introduce the panels into the literature for the first time, and his very detailed descriptions open the way for more study. The book had a wide influence on future reporters.

1784 Hunter, William, "An Account of Some Artificial Caverns in the Neighbourhood of Bombay," *Archaeologia*, vol. VII, 286, London, 1784.
Hunter describes the panels and the architectural elements in great detail and systematically, although with some personal ambivalence between his aversion and his admiration for the mastery of the art.

1783 Macneil, Hector, "An Account of the Caves of Canara, Ambola, and Elephanta in the East Indies," letter to a friend in England, dated 1783 and communicated by the Rev. Mr. Gregory, *Archaeologia*, vol. VIII, 251.
Macneil is of the opinion that it was not the soldiers but the Portuguese authorities who were responsible for the destruction. He reports seeing a long inscription in Persian characters "on the side of one of the doors that lead to the grand cave." He expressed bewilderment concerning the forms.

1799 Daniell, Thomas, *Oriental Scenery: Views of Agra, Delhi and of Elephanta and Salsette*, London, 1799.
Master engravers present their works including one of the entrance to the cave and one of part of the interior, showing the condition of the cave at this time.

1799 Goldingham, —, *Asiatic Researches*, vol. IV, 411, London, 1801.
Accurate measurements and ground plan as well as a picture of the Eternal Shiva are presented.

Nineteenth-Century Accounts

1803 Valentia, Viscount G., *Voyages and Travels to India*, vol. II, 1809, 199-200.
This is a general account.

1806 Maurice's *Indian Antiquities or Dissertations*, vol. II, London, 1806, 125-170.

Maurice takes his information from Fryer, Ovington, Grose, Hunter, Linschoten, and Niebuhr. He provides the possibly true information that the Mohammedans and Portuguese plastered the panels, and the defacement of stones is due to the Maratha's removal of the plaster. More speculations concerning origins.

1812 Graham, Maria, *Journal of a Residence in India*, 2d ed., Edinburgh, 1813, pp. 54-59.

This is a general report of a day's visit, with amateur drawings.

1812 Forbes, —, *Oriental Memoirs*, vol. I, 2d ed., pp. 270-274.

Forbes, a writer for the East India Company, gives a general description.

1812 Ouseley, Sir William, *Travels in the East*, vol. I, London, 1819.

This presentation indulges in general speculation and is primarily important for Major D'Arcy's drawing, later made into a fine engraving, which reveals the state of the cave at this time.

1813 Erskine, William, "Account of the Cave-Temple of Elephanta with a plan and drawings of the principal figures," *Transactions of the Literary Society of Bombay*, vol. I, London, 1819, read Nov. 2, 1813, 214.

This is a very important monograph compiled during a ten-day retreat in the cave. Accurate and detailed descriptions and measurements along with a new understanding of the iconography make it the first really useful guide. Mrs. Ashburner is also the first artist to draw from the panels directly. Accurate and subtle rendering of details gives a true idea of the panels for the first time.

1813 Hall, Captain Basil, *Fragments of Voyages and Travels*, vol. III, 192-281.

This is a very delightful account of the ten-day sojourn of a group of friends, which included Erskine, Mrs. Ashburner, the engineer who made the ground plans, and others, which resulted in Erskine's report, composed in the cave with the cooperation of the entire group.

1819 Fitzclarence, Lt. Col., *Journal of a Route Across India*, London, 1819, p. 321.

An unenthusiastic visitor doubts that the Portuguese were responsible for the damage.

1828 Heber, R., *Narrative of a Journey through the Upper Provinces of India*, vol. II, 1828, 136.

This is an appreciative general description with details concerning the deteriorated state of the cave.

1845 Fergusson, James, *Illustrations of the Rock Cut Temples of India*, London, 1845, pp. 54-55.

Elephanta is not included in the illustrations. Fergusson gives a general description, agreeing with Erskine that Eternal Shiva is not the triad of Brahma, Vishnu, Shiva.

1847 Wilson, John, "Memoir on the Cave Temples and Monasteries and Other Ancient

Buddhist, Brahmanical and Jaina remains of Western India," *Journal of the Bombay Branch of the Royal Asiatic Society*, vol. III, pt. II, 1847, 41.
Dr. Wilson offers brief remarks.

1850 ———, "Second Memoir on the Cave Temples and Monasteries and Other Ancient Buddhist, Brahmanical and Jaina remains of Western India," *Journal of the Bombay Branch of the Royal Asiatic Society*, vol. IV, 1850, 341-342.
Wilson reports the finding of the leographs in the East Court and discovers the link to Ellora.

1852 Stevenson, J., "The Theory of the Great Elephanta Cave," *Journal of the Bombay Branch of the Royal Asiatic Society*, vol. IV, no. XVI, 1850-1852, 261-275.
This is a good guide with Puranic references.

1857 Falkland, The Viscountess, *Selections from a Journal kept in India, Egypt, and Syria, Chow-Chow et al.*, vol. I, 108-114, London, 1857.
An intrepid traveler gives a general description.

1866 Wilson, John, "The Religious Excavations of Western India," *Calcutta Review*, vol. XLII, 1866.
Wilson gives another brief description of some of the panels.

1880 Fergusson, James, and James Burgess, *The Cave Temples of India*, London, 1880, pp. 465-475.
This is a general review of material in Burgess' monograph of Elephanta.

Guide Books (If not annotated, the work is not important.)

1884 *Pearse's Guide to Elephanta (or Gharapuri)*, 1884.

1892 Carpenter, Edward, *From Adam's Peak to Elephanta*, London, 1892.
This is valuable for the photographs showing the condition of the cave at this time.

n.d. Harris, —, *Historical and Descriptive Guide to the Rock Cut Caves of Elephanta.*

1911 *A Guide to Elephanta Island*, published in 1911 for the visit of King George V and Queen Mary.

1912 Rousselet, L., *Wonders of the World*, London, 1912, pp. 218-225.

n.d. Bhandarkar, D. R., *Guide to Elephanta Island.*

1914 Bombay Public Works Department, *Caves of Elephanta.*

1931 Gladstone, Solomon E., *The Art of Elephanta*, Bombay, 1931.

1932 Vakil, Kanaiyalal H., *Rock Cut Temples Around Bombay at Elephanta, Jogeshwari, Mandapeshwar and Kanheri*, D. B. Taraporevala Sons and Co., 1932.
This is a substantial, 160-page guide. The sensitive author makes a plea for a fresh approach that will evaluate the aesthetics of the cave as opposed to the publication of repetitive descriptions. There are interesting quotations from literature and revealing contemporary photographs.

1957 Chandra, Pramod, *A Guide to the Elephanta Caves*, Bhulabhai Memorial Institute, Ancient Monuments of India, Bombay, 1957.

An excellent, in-depth description with fold-out illustration, ground plan, and revealing photographs.

Recent Publications

1935 Sarasvati, Sarasi, review of Sastri, Hirananda, *A Guide to Elephanta*, in *Journal of the Indian Society of Oriental Art*, vol. III, no. 1, June 1935.

Sarasvati contributes the idea that the three-headed figure at the top of the Gangadharamurti panel represents Ganga in her threefold form of Mandakini, Suradhaṇi and Bhagavati.

1946 Kramrisch, Stella, "The Image of Mahadeva in the Cave-Temple on Elephanta Island," *Ancient India*, no. 2, 1946, p. 4.

Citing sources, Dr. Kramrisch explains the symbolic significance of the Mahadeva as *pancha mukha linga*, the five faces of Shiva, with Tatpurusha, Aghora, and Vamadeva actualized at Elephanta.

1955 Banerjea, J. N., "The So-Called Trimurti of Elephanta," *Arts Asiatiques*, II, 1955, 124.

Banerjea argues that the face on the left is Uma, female, symbolizing the union of male and female in Shiva, a syncretist image showing two forms of Shiva and one of Shakti.

1955 Chakravarti, S. N., "The Image of Brahma from Elephanta," *Lalit Kala*, vols. 1 and 2, 1955, 87-89.

The author identifies a four-faced freestanding statue found at the entrance of the main cave as Brahma and not Sadashiva.

1955 Zimmer, H., *The Art of Indian Asia*, New York, 1955, vol. II, pls. 248-265.

Eighteen beautiful photographs by Eliot Elsofon for the first time reveal and expose the internal relationships of space and sculptures to public view. The statues are understood and shown to be great works of art.

1958 Gangoli, O. C., *The Art of the Rashtrakutas*, Longmans, pp. 25-26, pls. 35-40.

Six large plates illustrate a thesis that the panels were of Rashtrakuta patronage.

1960 "Elephanta," *Marg*, September 1960, vol. XIII, no. 4.

In this, the most comprehensive study since Burgess, Mulk Raj Anand offers historical background, metaphysical groundings, and stylistic analysis. Muriel Neff, in two articles, considers first the architecture and then the style and iconography of the sculpture including comparisons with other caves. Dr. Rudy von Leyden traces the development of the style and for the first time recognizes stylistic differences between the panels. Photographs, mostly by Stella Snead and some by R. Bharadwaj, follow the Elsofon tradition.

1961 Soundara Rajan, K. V., review of the *Marg* issue in *Lalit Kala*, vol. 7, no. 9, April 1961, 64-65.

Dr. Soundara Rajan offers his views concerning the caves and comments on particular aspects of the *Marg* issue.

Gupte, R. S., "The Dating of the Elephanta Caves," *Journal of Indian History*, vol. XLIII, pt. II, August 1965, 513-530.

Dr. Gupte reviews all and then refutes some previous assumptions concerning the date of the cave. With the aid of epigraphical, stylistic, and iconographical evidence, he himself arrives at the conclusion that the Chalukyas of Badami, sometime between 600 A.D. and 645 A.D., were responsible for the excavation.

1971 Chaturvedi, S. N., "A Note on the Mahadeva Image of Elephanta," *Bulletin of Museums and Archeology in U. P.*, December 1971, p. 11.

This offers further comments on textual references to the five faces of Shiva, *pancha mukha linga*, with photographs showing the development from the single to the multiple faces on the *linga*.

1973 Mankodi, Kirit, "Ganga Tripathaga," *Artibus Asiae*, vol. XXXV, 139.

The three heads in the Gangadharamurti panel are identified as Ganga moving through the three worlds: *Mandakini*, the world of gods; *Bhagirathi*, the world of men; and *Bhogavati*, the underworld.

1976 Rau, Heimo, "Structural Plan and Stylistic Design of the Mahesha Cave Temple on Elephanta," in *Reflections on Indian Art*, Bombay, 1976, pp. 74-86.

This is the best overall introduction. The iconography of the cave is described sensitively and with accuracy. Rau speaks of the "opposite pictorial sermons" and "repeated pairs of opposites." Commenting on the composition, he posits the idea of three masters and three styles. Relationships with other sites are shown.

1977 Parimoo, Ratan, "Elephanta in the Context of Evolution and Significance of Saiva Culture," *Journal of the Oriental Institute*, vol. XXVI, no. 3, March 1977, 282. (Reprint, with Hirnanda Sastri's 1934 guide, New Delhi, 1978.)

Dr. Parimoo reviews the material on the *pancha mukha linga*, discusses iconographical identification, style, and composition in connection with definitions in contemporary sacred literature. He traces stylistic development from earlier times and particularly from Ajanta painting and Gupta sculpture. This is the beginning of a critical approach to style.

1981 Kramrisch, Stella, "The Great Cave Temple of Siva on the Island of Elephanta," in *The Presence of Siva*, Princeton, 1981, pp. 443-468, with 25 black and white plates by P. C. Patel.

With consummate, systematic discipline and inspired rhythmic prose, Dr. Kramrisch unfolds spellbinding revelations concerning the nature of Shiva in all his aspects. The reader is thus prepared for the encounter with the cave in the last chapter, wherein the author examines style, symbol, and myth and arrives at a final integration.

In press Spink, Walter M., "The Great Cave at Elephanta: A Study of Sources," in Bardwell Smith, ed., on Gupta art, in press, Varanasi.

Connections of Elephanta with Jogeshwari are established; the paintings at Ajanta are compared to Elephanta's panels. Later Dr. Spink offers numismatic evidence and cave comparisons as well as extensive references to Dandin's *Dasakumara-carita* to establish a mid-sixth-century date under the patronage of the early Kalacuri king Krsnaraja.

Deshpande, B. S., and R. S. Gupte, "Dating of the Elephanta, Mandapeshwar and Jogeshwari Caves," *Bulletin of the Prince of Wales Museum of Western India*, no. 13 (Dr. Moti Chandra Commemoration volume), in press.

Spink, Walter M., "Elephanta: Relationship with Ajanta and Ellora," *Bulletin of the Prince of Wales Museum of Western India*, no. 13 (Dr. Moti Chandra Commemoration volume), in press.

References Relating to the Sadashiva Symbolism

1914 Rao, Gopinath, *Elements of Hindu Iconography*, 2 vols., Madras, 1914, vol. 2, pt. 1, 361-411; reprint, 1971.

1975 Khumar, Krishna, "A Dhyanayoga Mahesamurti and Some Reflections on the Mahesamurti Images," *Artibus Asiae*, vol. XXXVIII, nos. 1-2, 1975.

1976 Sharma, B. N., *Iconography of Sadasiva*, New Delhi, 1976.

1976 Sivaramamurti, C., *Satarudriya: Vibhuti of Siva's Iconography*, New Delhi, 1976.

Contributors

CARMEL BERKSON is a sculptor and photographer of Indian art who lives in Bombay. She is the author of recent articles in *Artibus Asiae, Marg,* and *Rupa Pratirupa.*

GEORGE MICHELL is the editor of *Art and Archaeology Research Papers* (London); author of *The Hindu Temple: An Introduction to Its Meaning and Forms* (New York: Harper, 1977); and editor of *Brick Temples of Bengal: From the Archives of David McCutchion* (Princeton: Princeton University Press, 1983).

WENDY DONIGER O'FLAHERTY is Professor of History of Religions at the University of Chicago and author of *Asceticism and Eroticism in the Mythology of Siva* (Oxford: Oxford University Press, 1973; New York, paperback, 1981); *Hindu Myths* (Harmondsworth: Penguin, 1975); *The Origins of Evil in Hindu Mythology* (Berkeley: University of California Press, 1976); *Women, Androgynes, and Other Mythical Beasts* (Chicago: University of Chicago Press, 1980); and *The Rig Veda: An Anthology* (Harmondsworth: Penguin, 1981).

While in general I have tried to reproduce what is seen by the naked eye as closely as possible, certain photographs suffer from distortion caused by using wide-angle lens from a side position.

PLATES

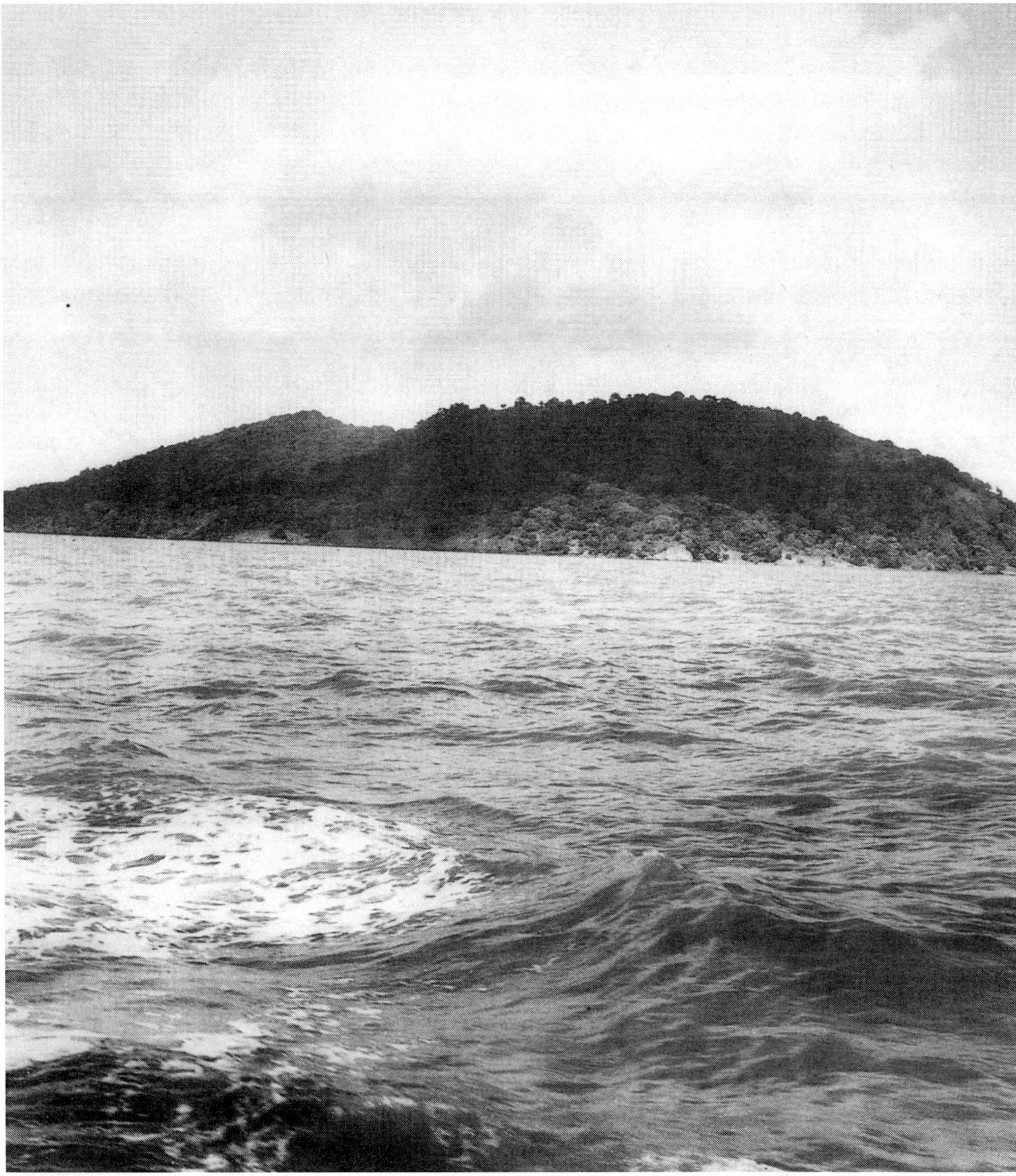

PL. 1. The island of Elephanta, approaching from the west.

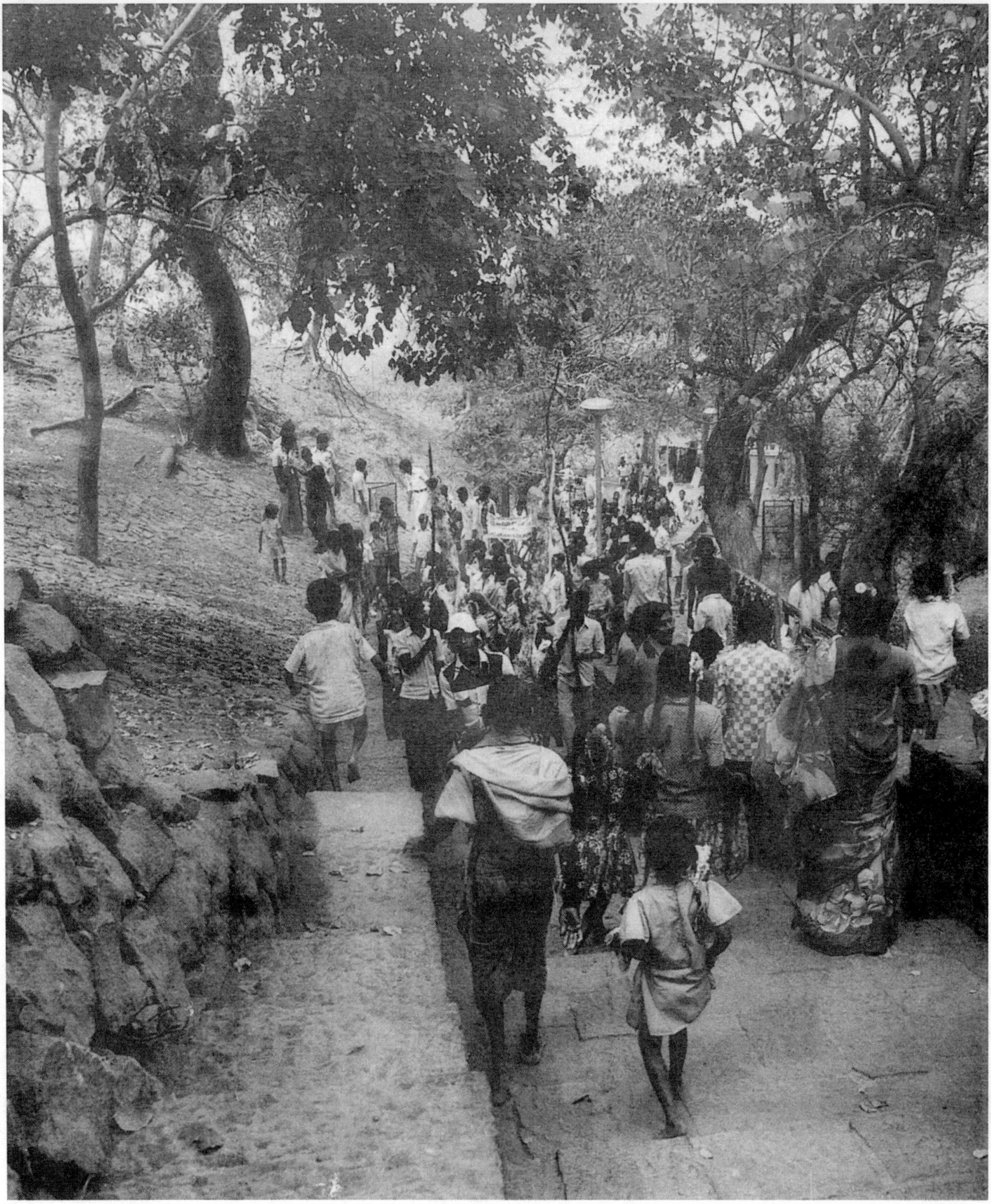

PL. 2. The ascent from the sea to the caves showing worshipers on Shivaratri day.

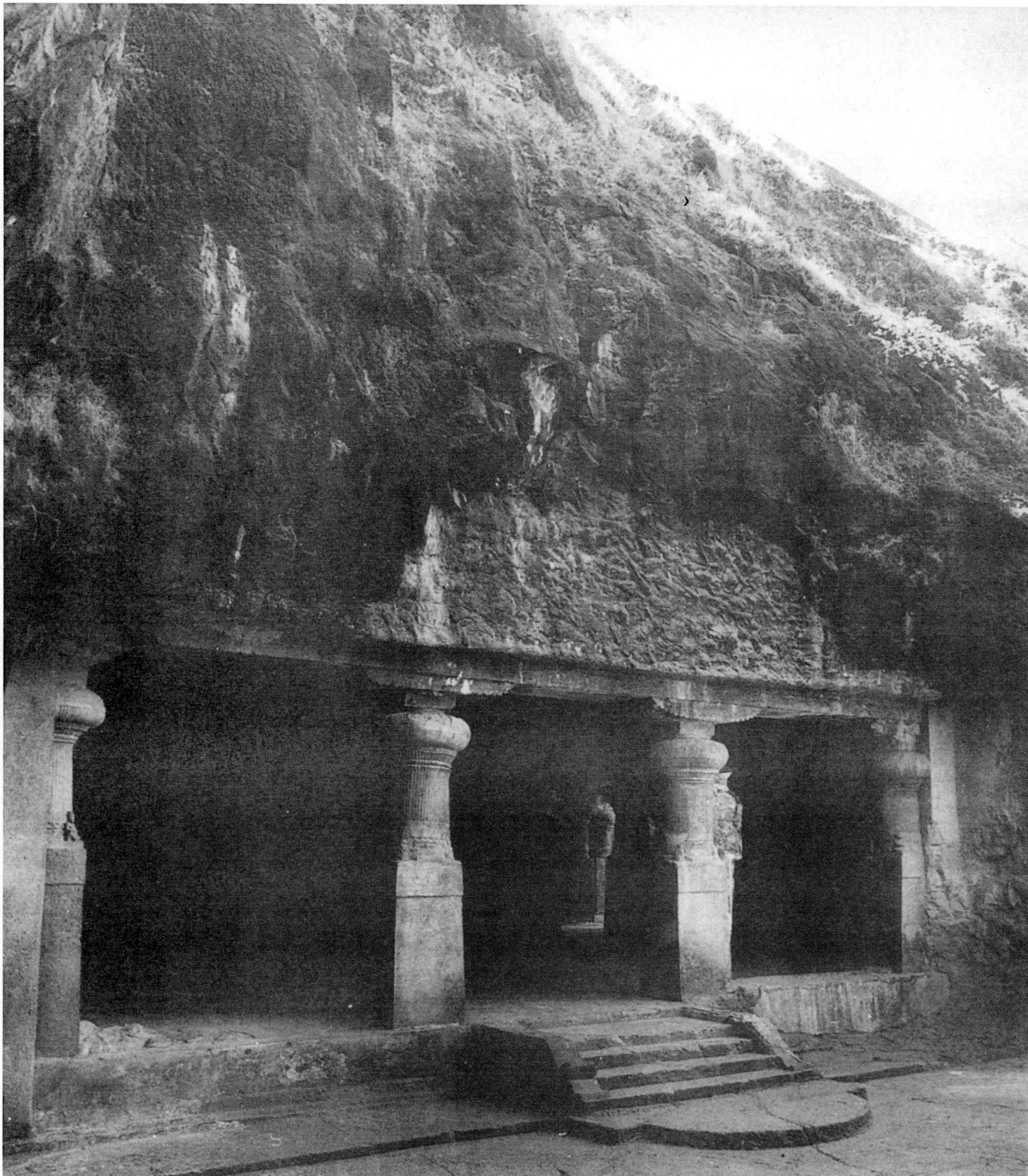

PL. 3. The east entrance to the cave; a view from the east court. This was probably the original primary entrance.

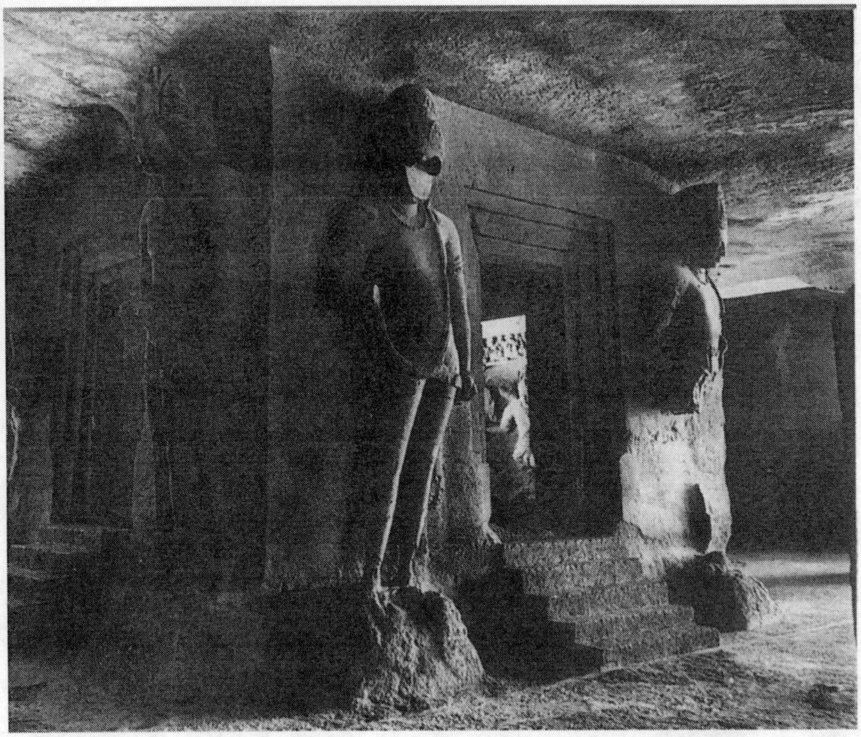

PL. 4. A view of the sanctum from the southeast, showing doorkeepers on the east and south walls, with partial view of Shiva in Andhakasura panel through the east and north doors.

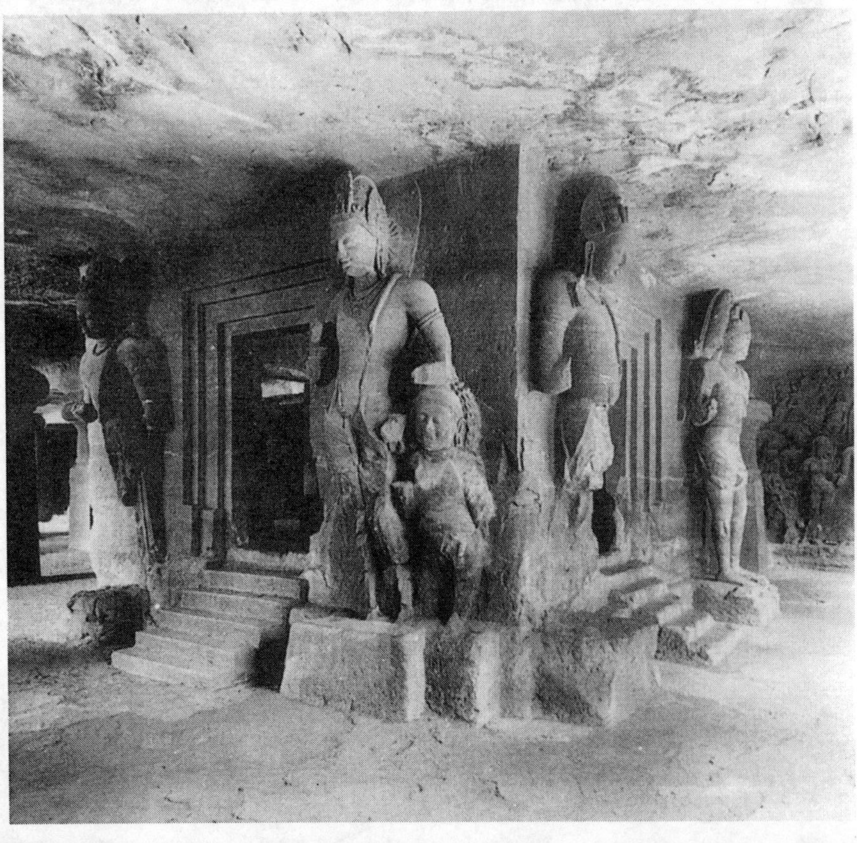

PL. 5. The sanctum from the northwest, showing the Marriage panel on the south wall.

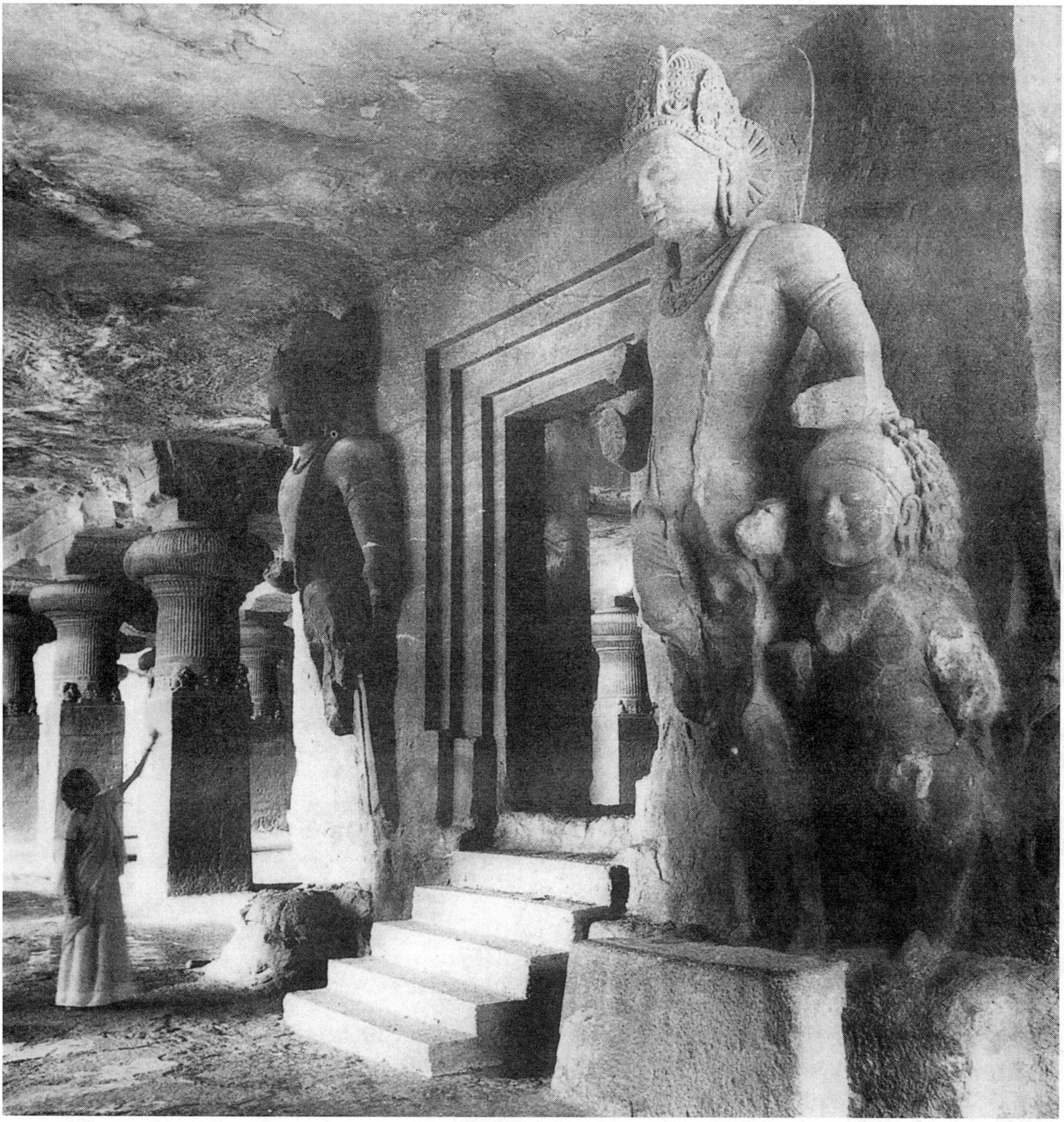

PL. 6. The north side of the sanctum from the northwest, with doorkeepers and dwarf.

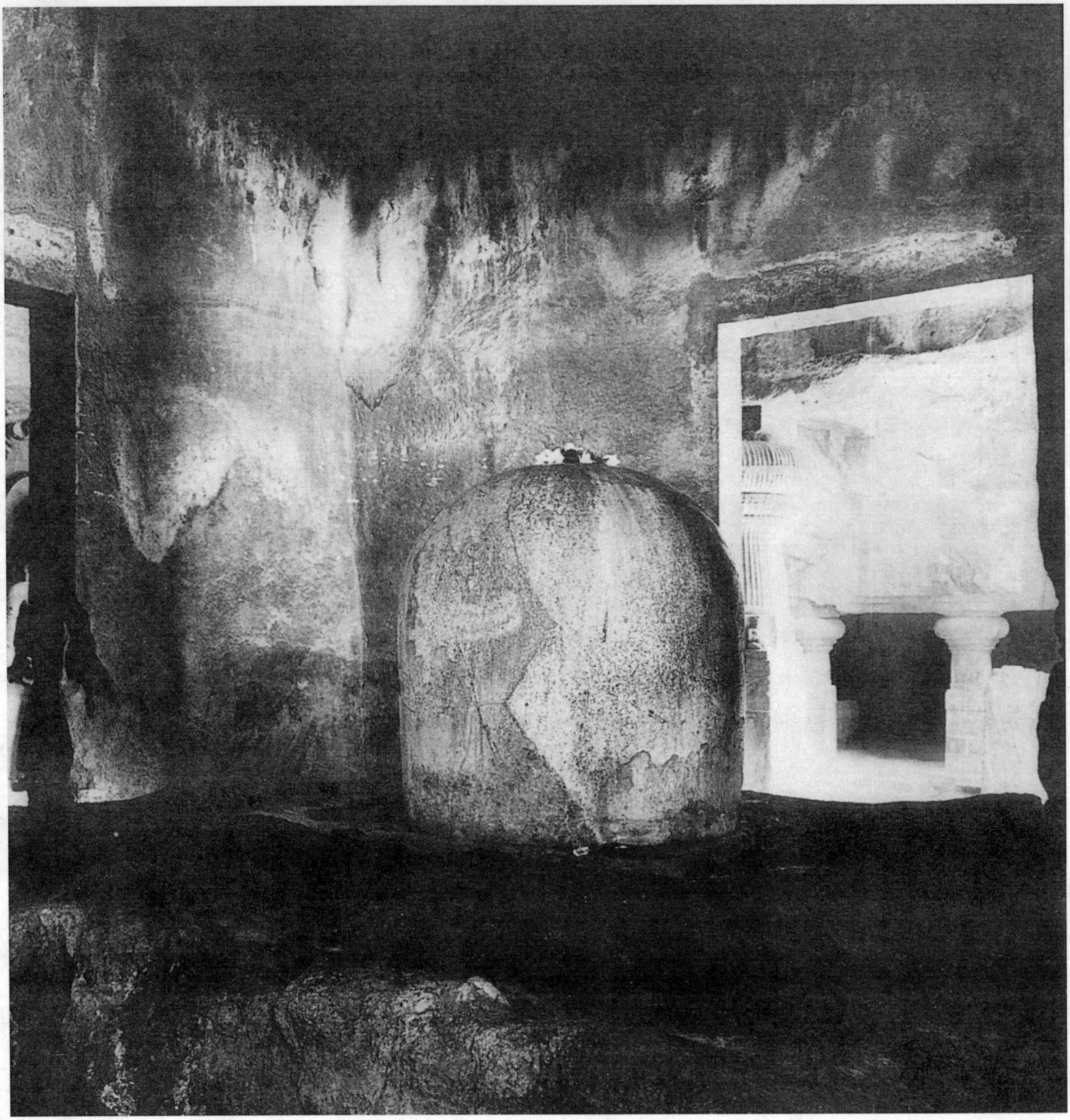

PL. 7. The *linga* and its pedestal in the sanctum, showing the figure of Parvati through the south door and the west wing shrine through the west door.

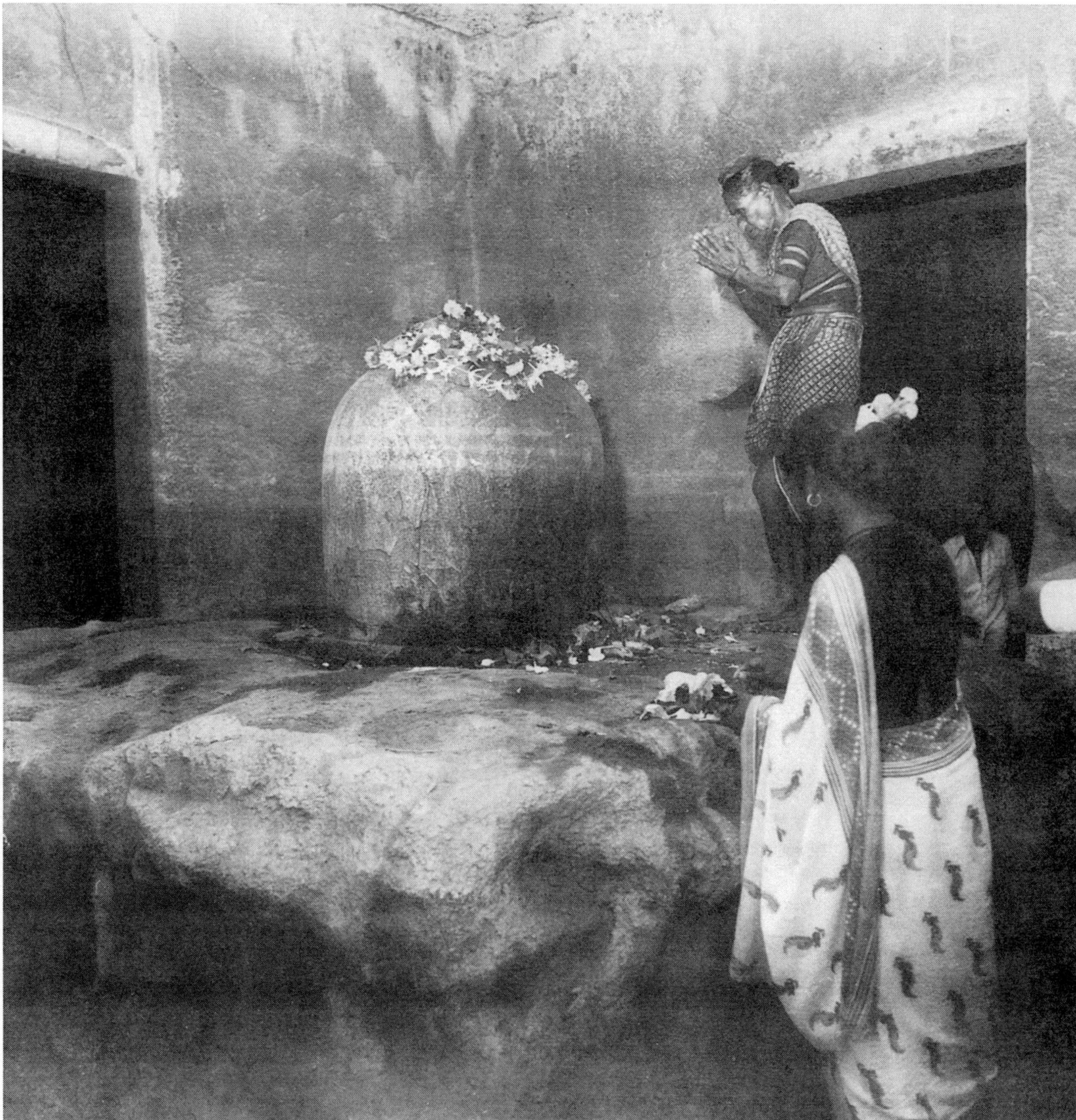

PL. 8. Two ladies worshiping the *linga* within the sanctum during the Shivaratri festival.

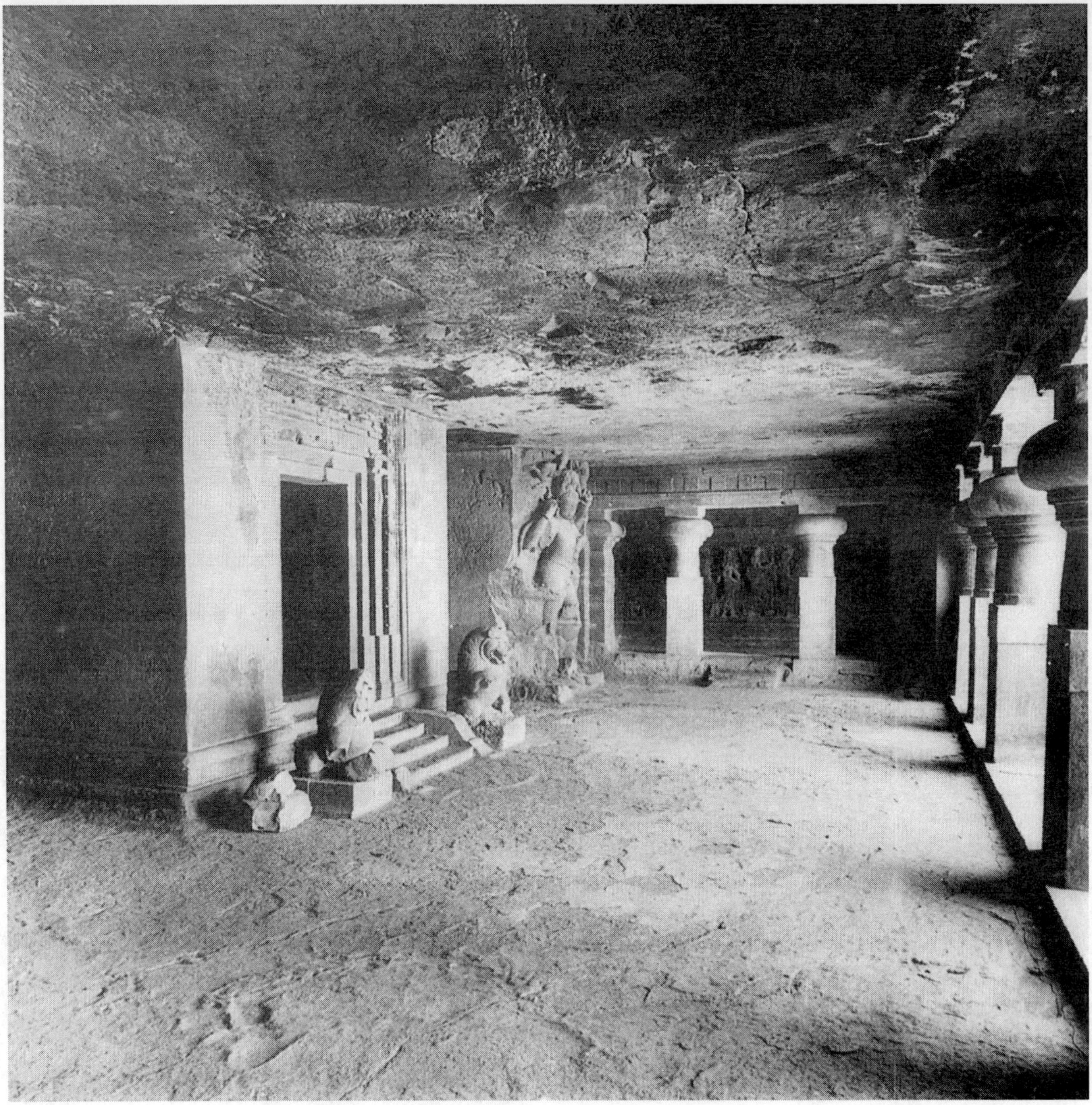

PL. 9. East wing shrine, the interior of the hall from the east with the Matrika chamber on the west, and the sanctum.

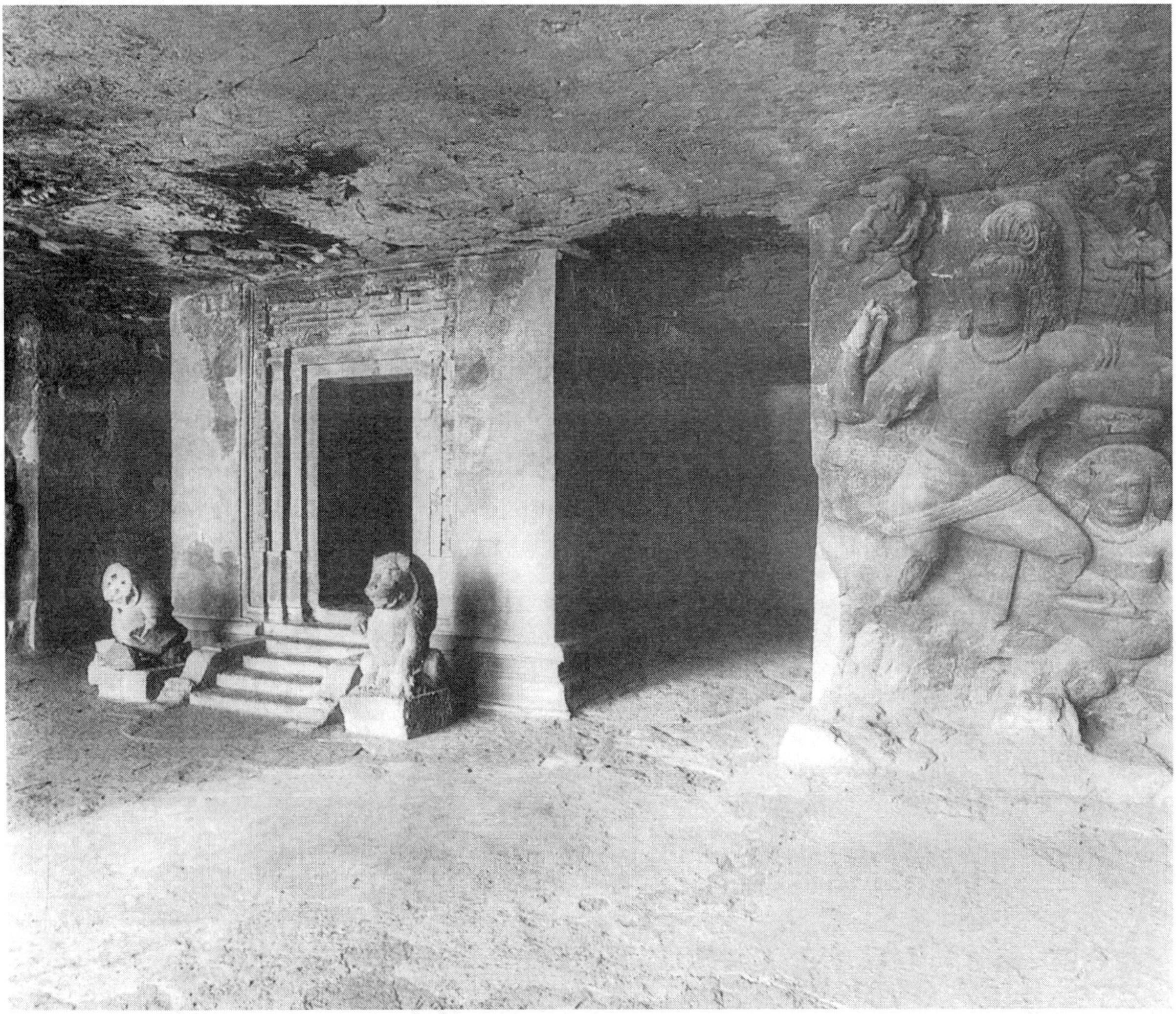

PL. 10. East wing shrine, the hall with Shiva *dvarapala* and dwarf and the sanctum fronted by two lions.

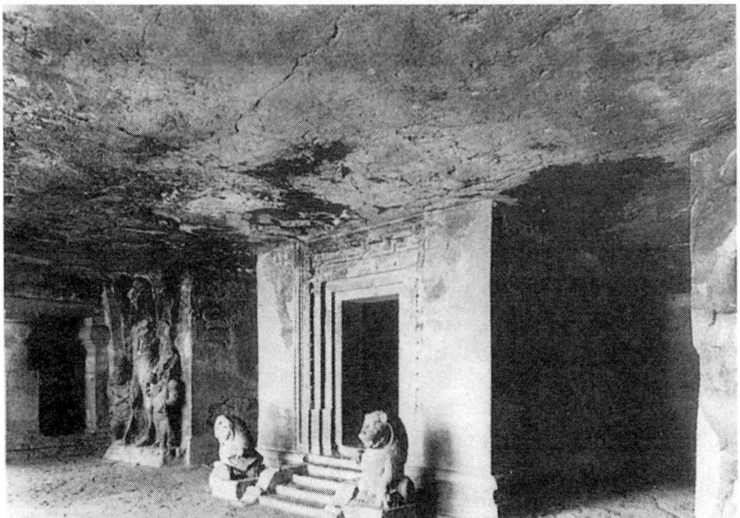

PL. 11. East wing shrine, the sanctum.

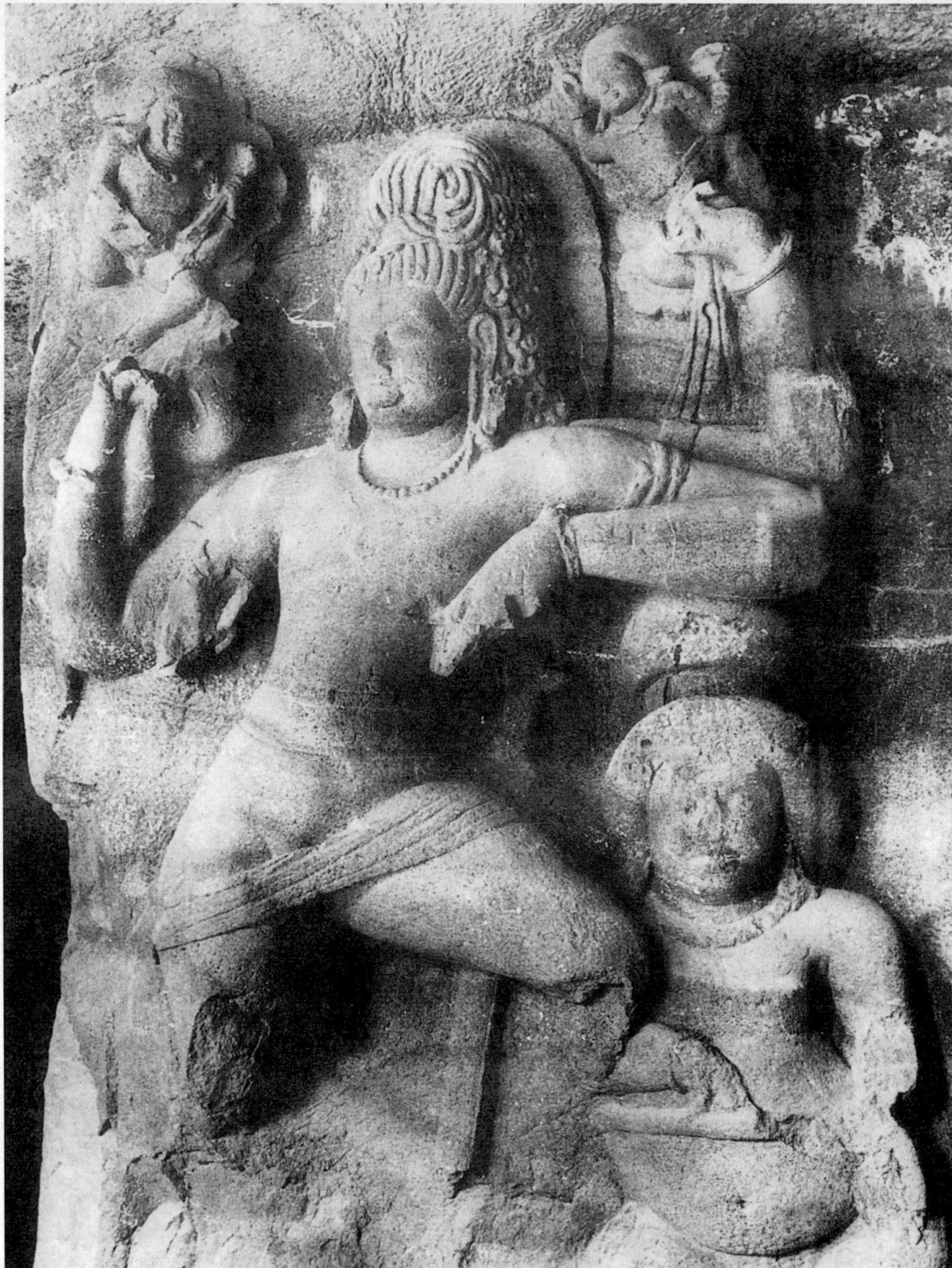

PL. 12. East wing shrine, Shiva *dvarapala*.

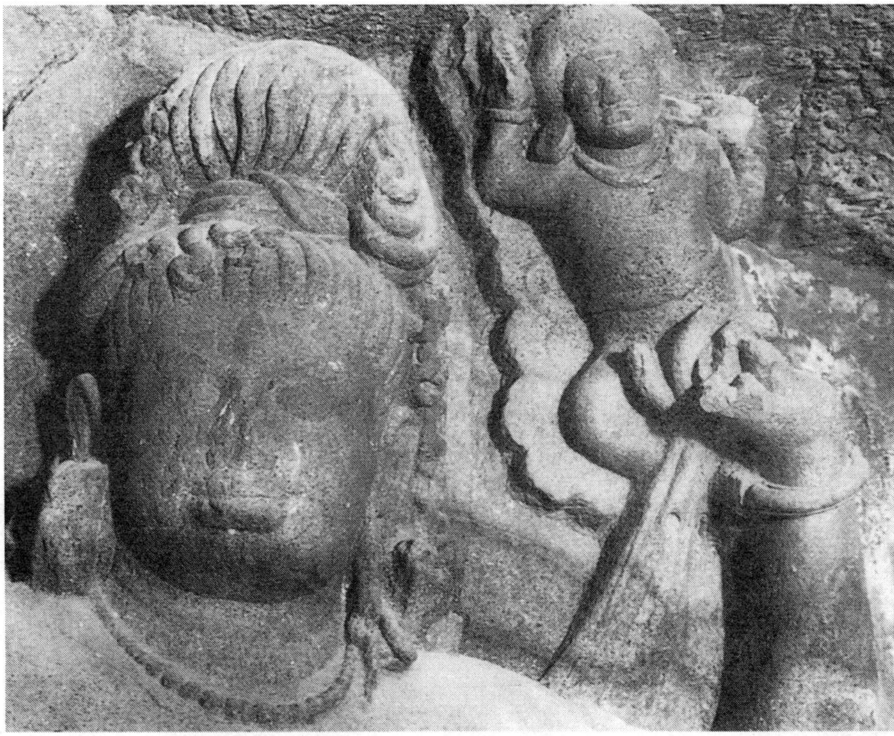

PL. 13. East wing shrine, Shiva *dvarapala,* detail.

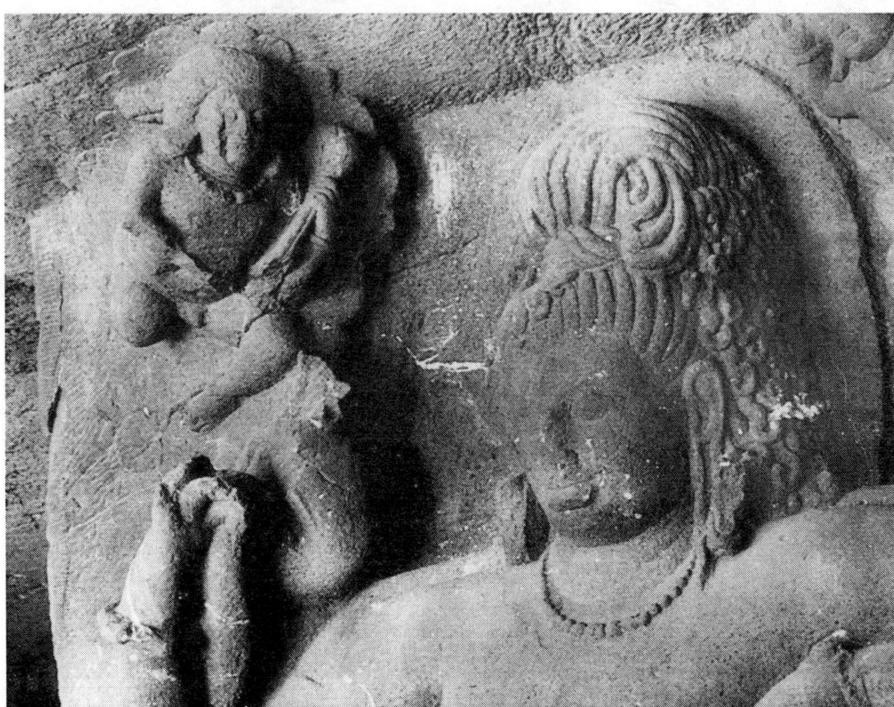

PL. 14. East wing shrine, Shiva *dvarapala,* detail.

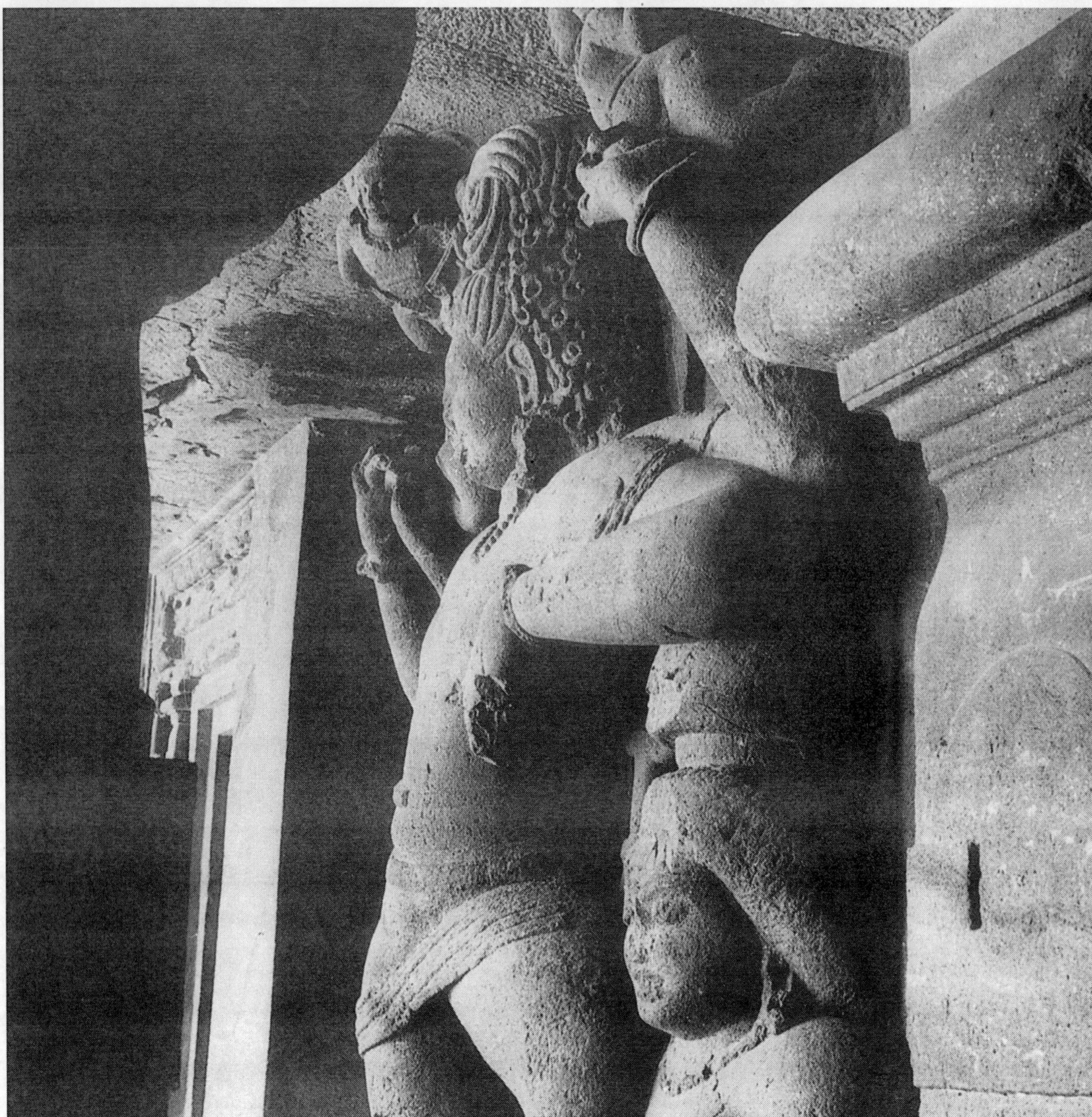

PL. 15. East wing shrine, Shiva *dvarapala,* view from chamber.

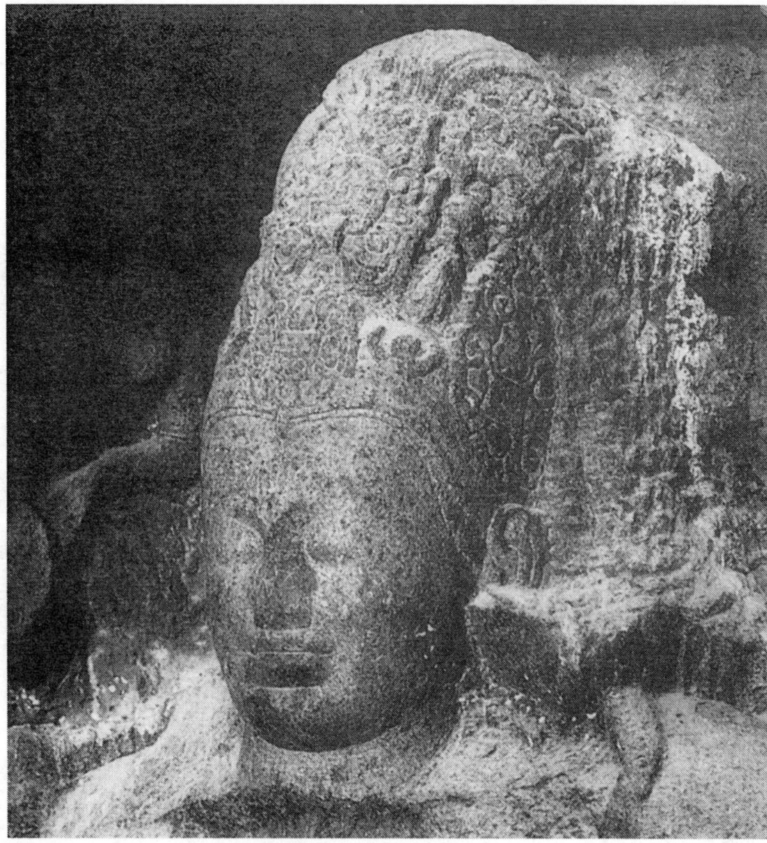

PL. 16. West wing shrine, Shiva Dancing (in *Lalita*), detail.

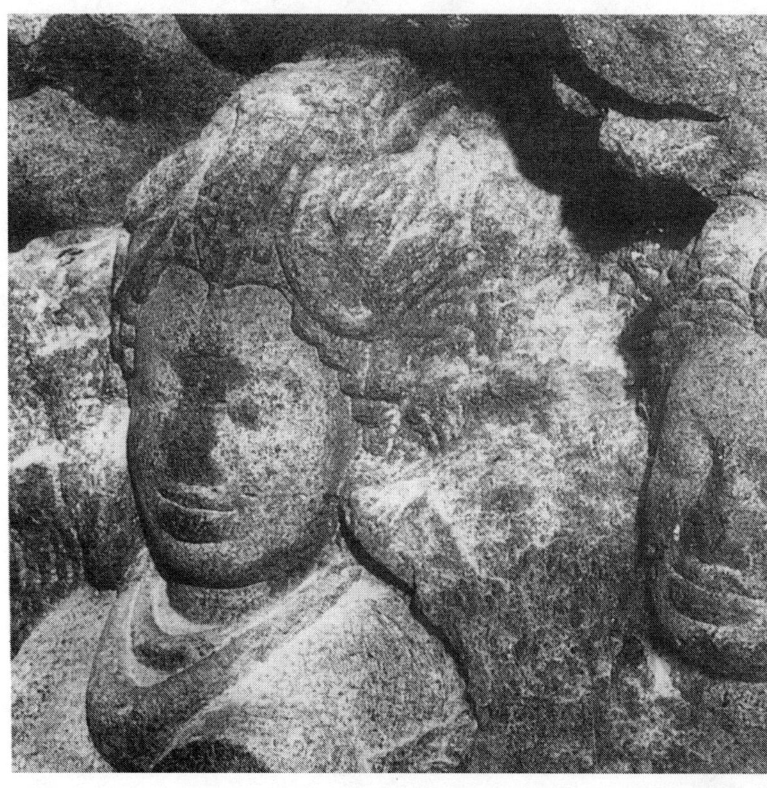

PL. 17. West wing shrine, female attendants (detail) Shiva Dancing (in *Lalita*).

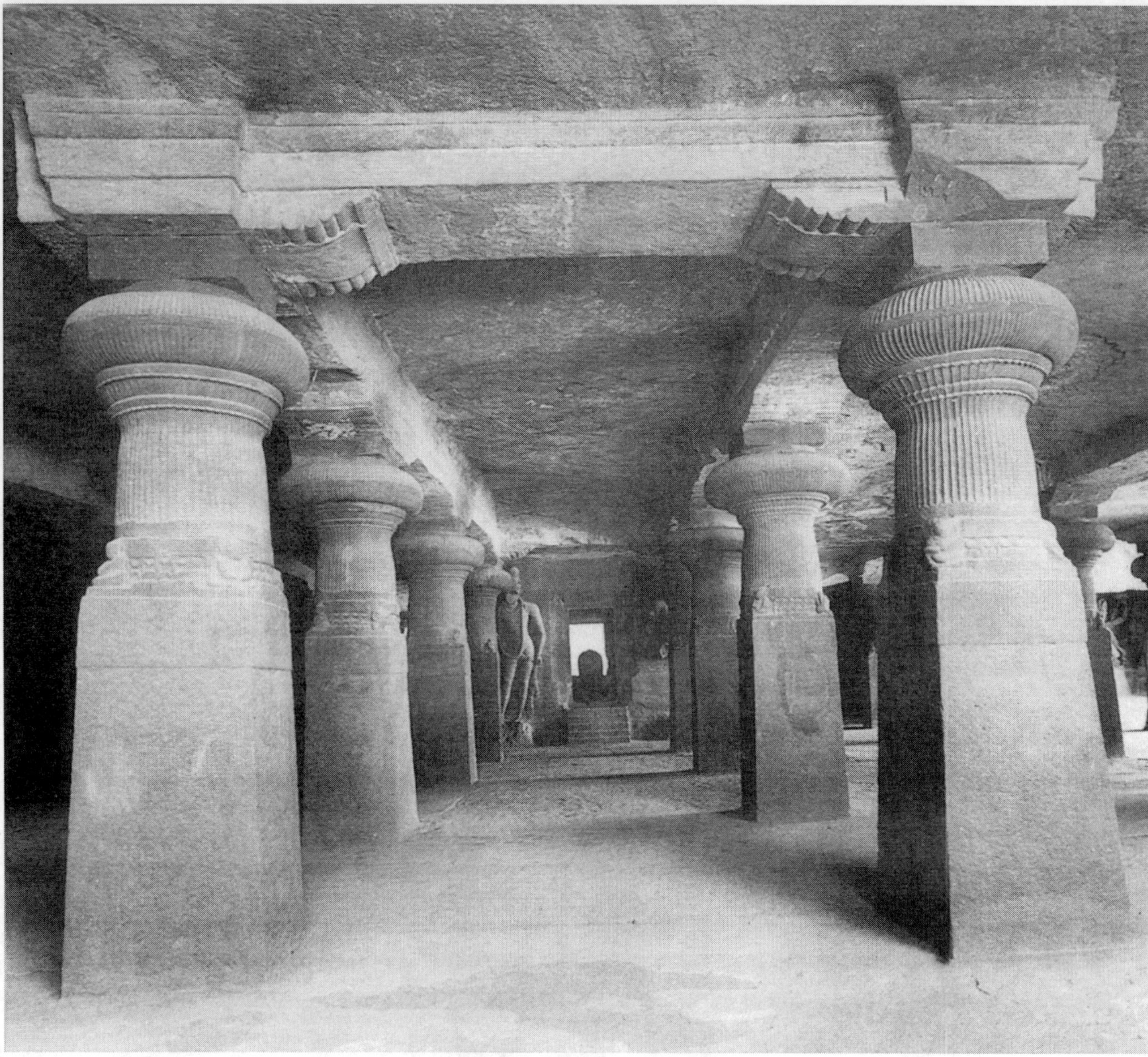

PL. 18. The *linga* in the sanctum, view from east entrance with false ceiling beams, defining this area as the hall.

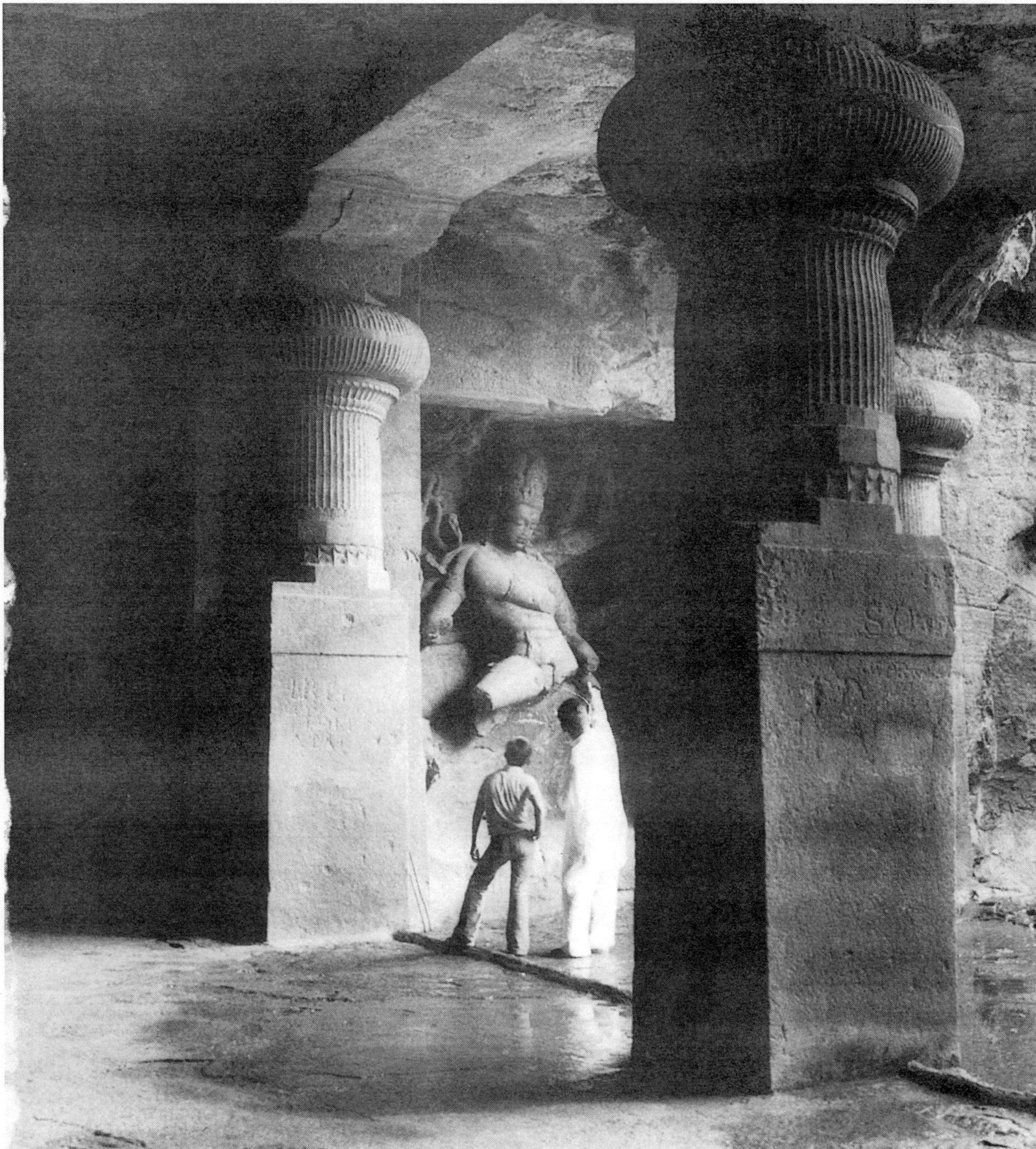

PL. 19. Shiva Dancing (in *Lalita*) panel, through columns.

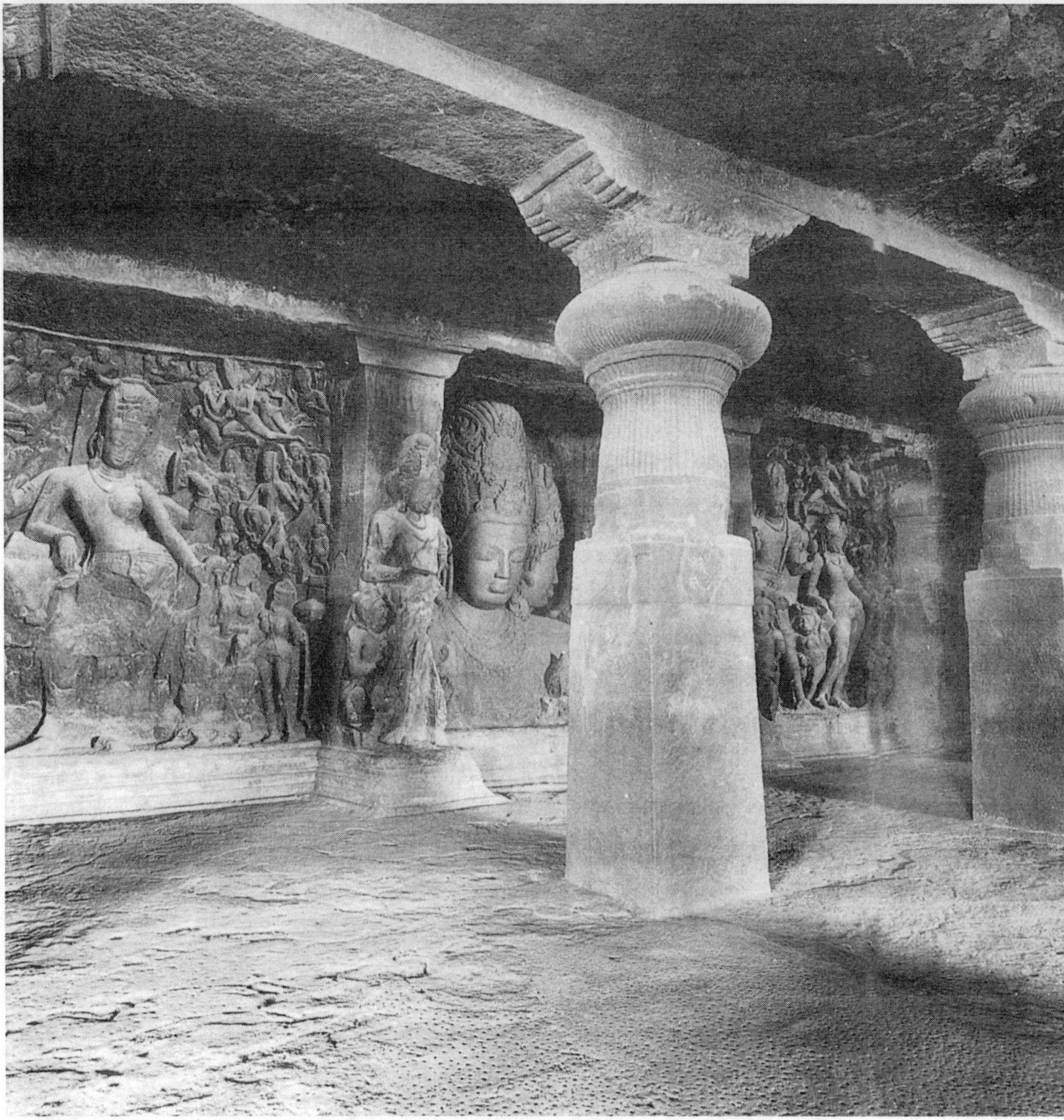

PL. 20. The south wall from the east showing the Androgyne, Eternal Shiva and (Descent of the) Ganges panels and the doorkeeper and dwarf to the right of Eternal Shiva.

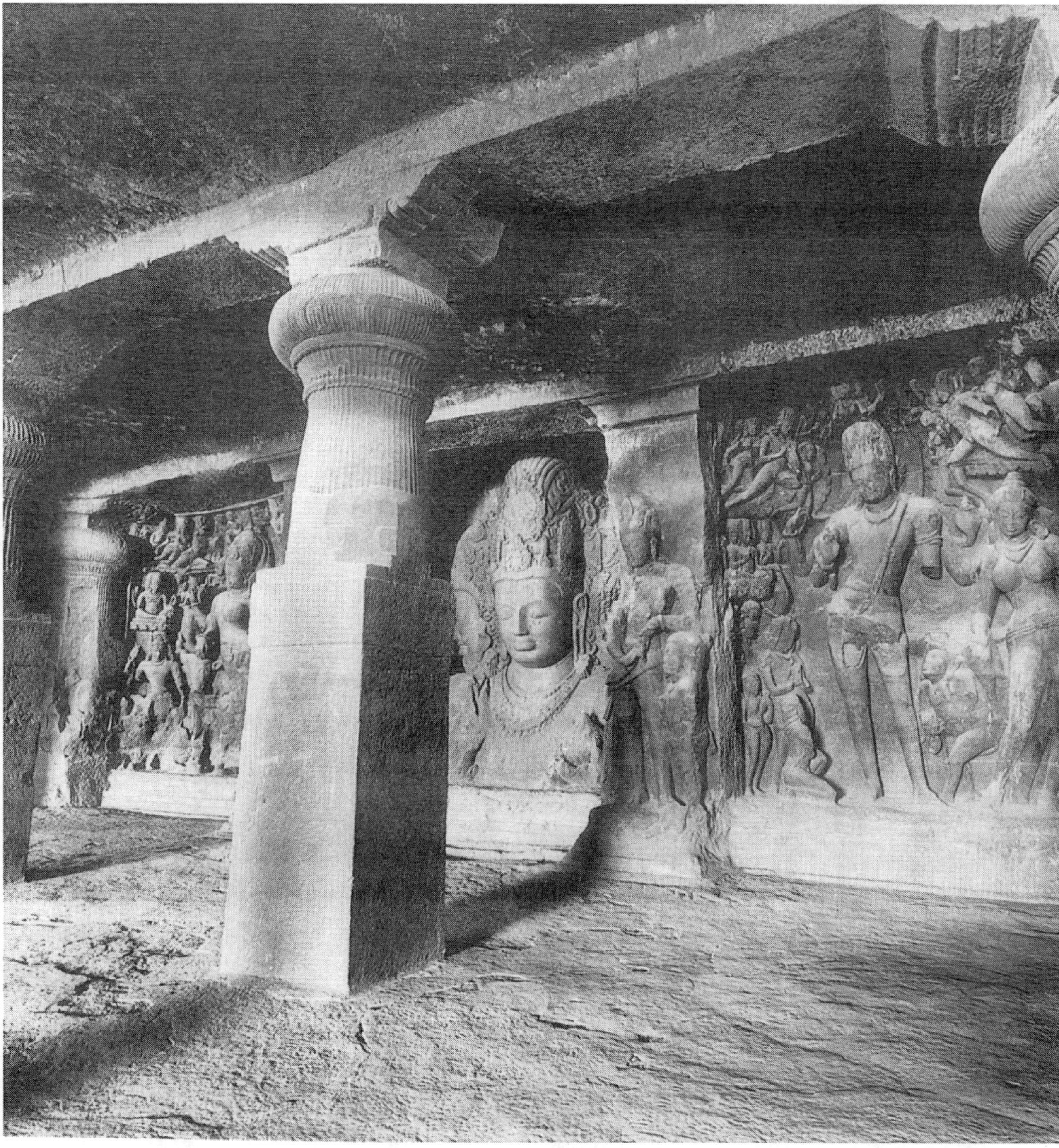

PL. 21. The south wall from the west showing (Descent of the) Ganges, Eternal Shiva, and the Androgyne panels, with the doorkeeper and dwarf to the left of Eternal Shiva.

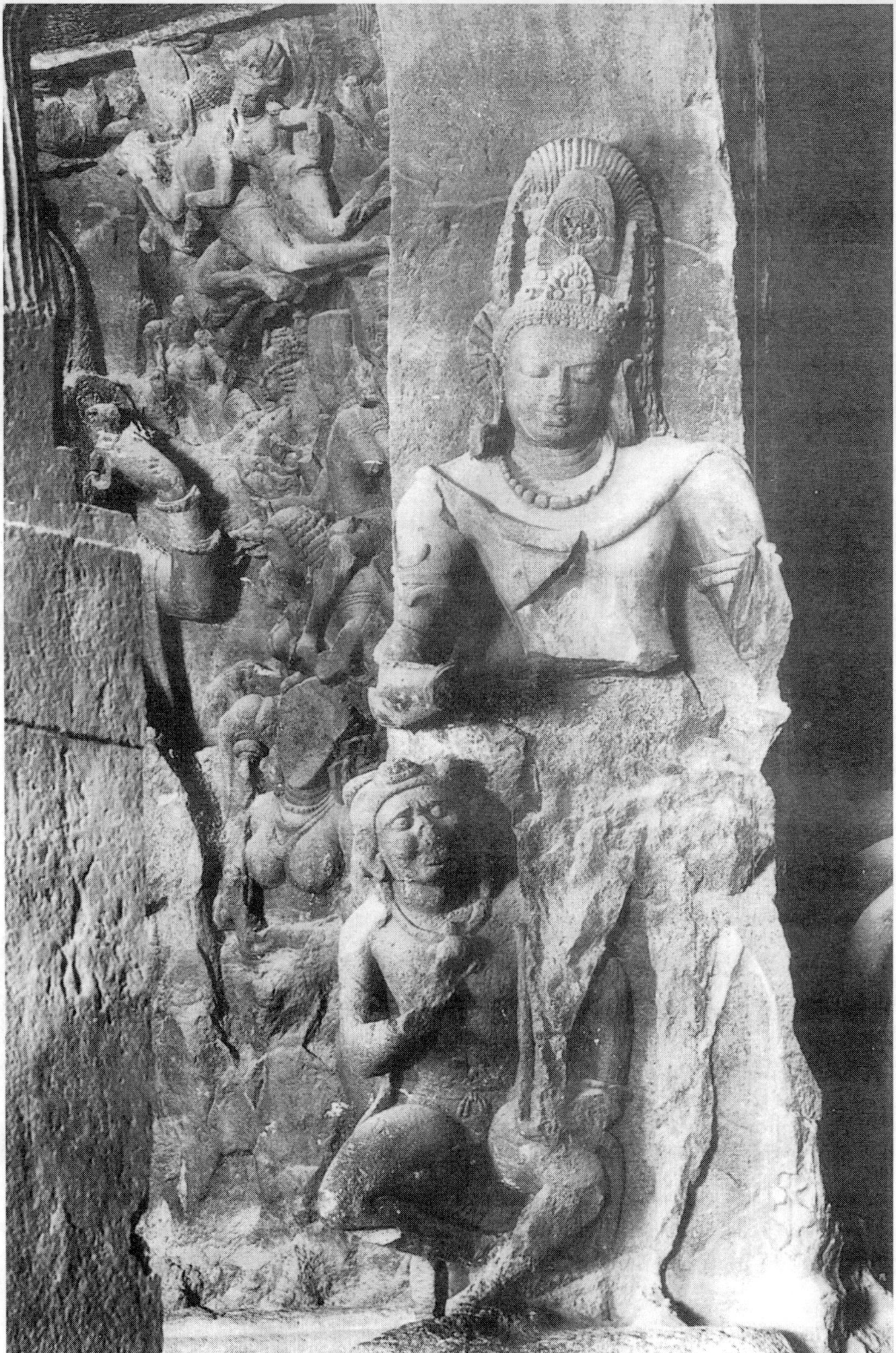

PL. 22. The doorkeeper and dwarf to the right of Eternal Shiva.

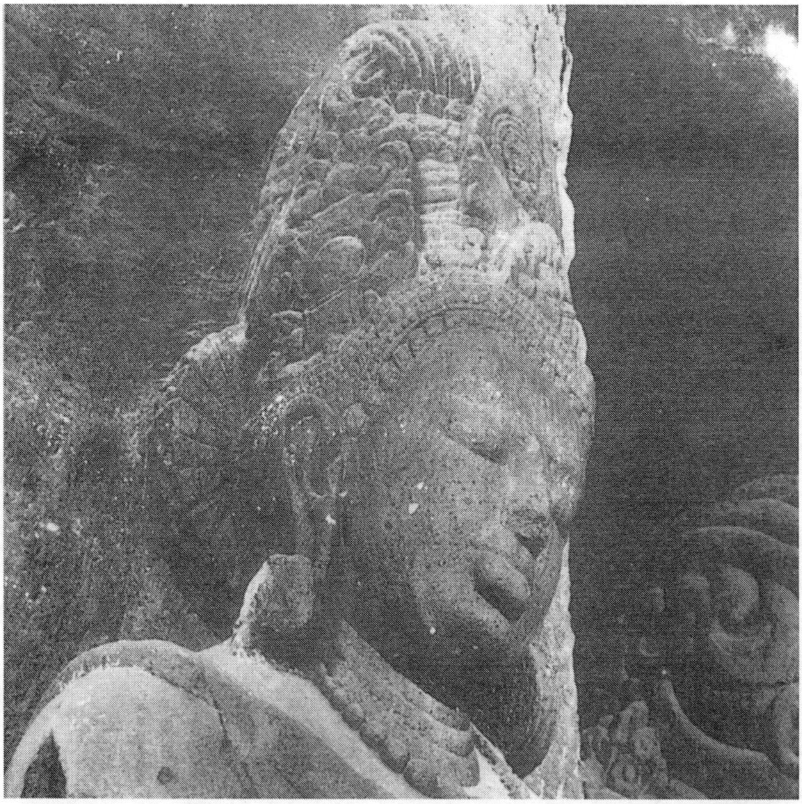

PL. 23. Detail of doorkeeper to the right of Eternal Shiva.

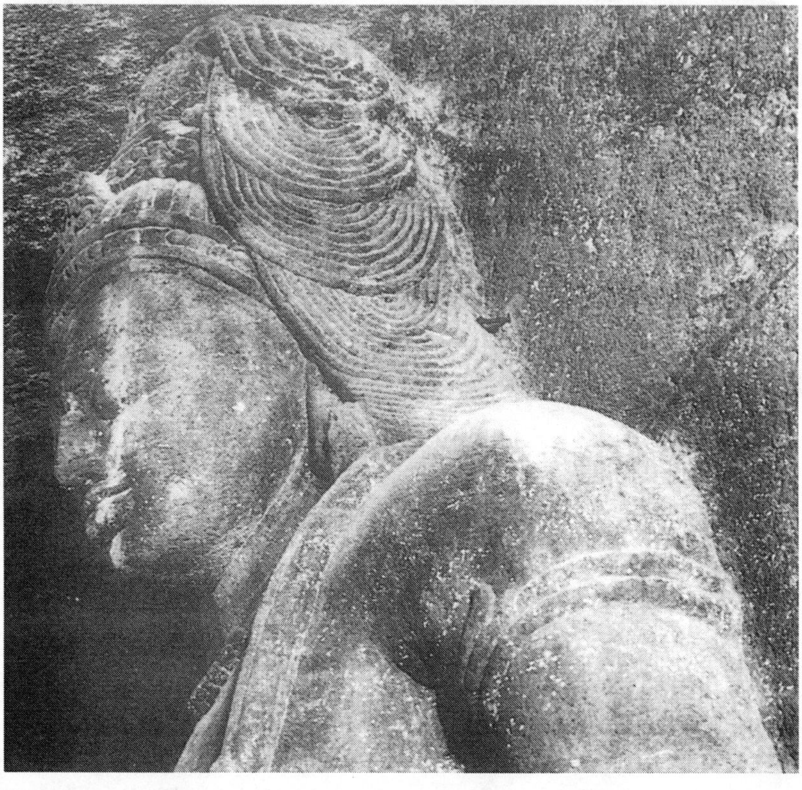

PL. 24. Detail of doorkeeper, east side of north wall of sanctum from the west.

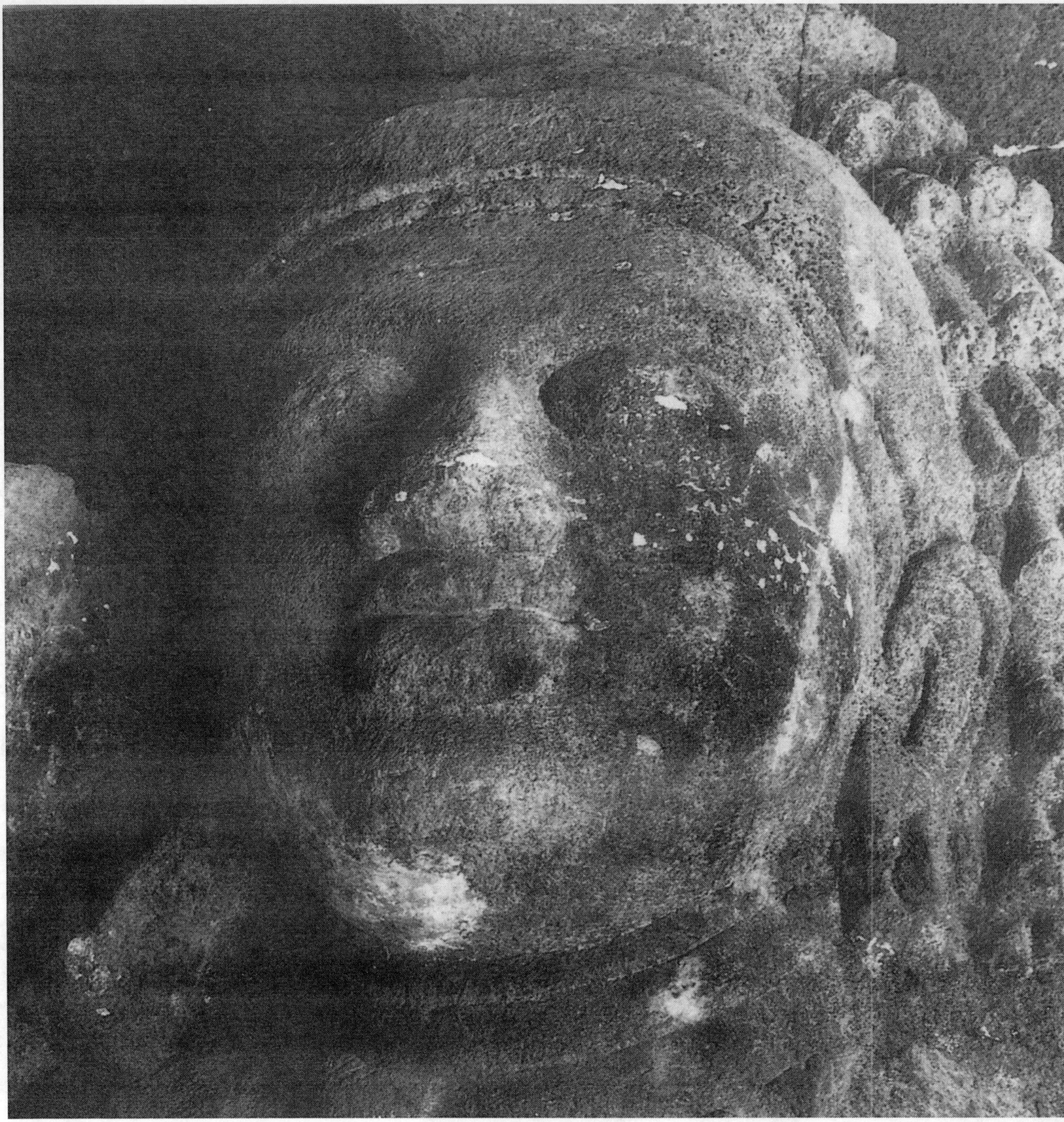

PL. 25. Detail of dwarf accompanying doorkeeper on north wall of sanctum, west of doorway.

PL. 26. (Opposite) Umamaheshvara—the Gambling Scene panel, east veranda, south side.

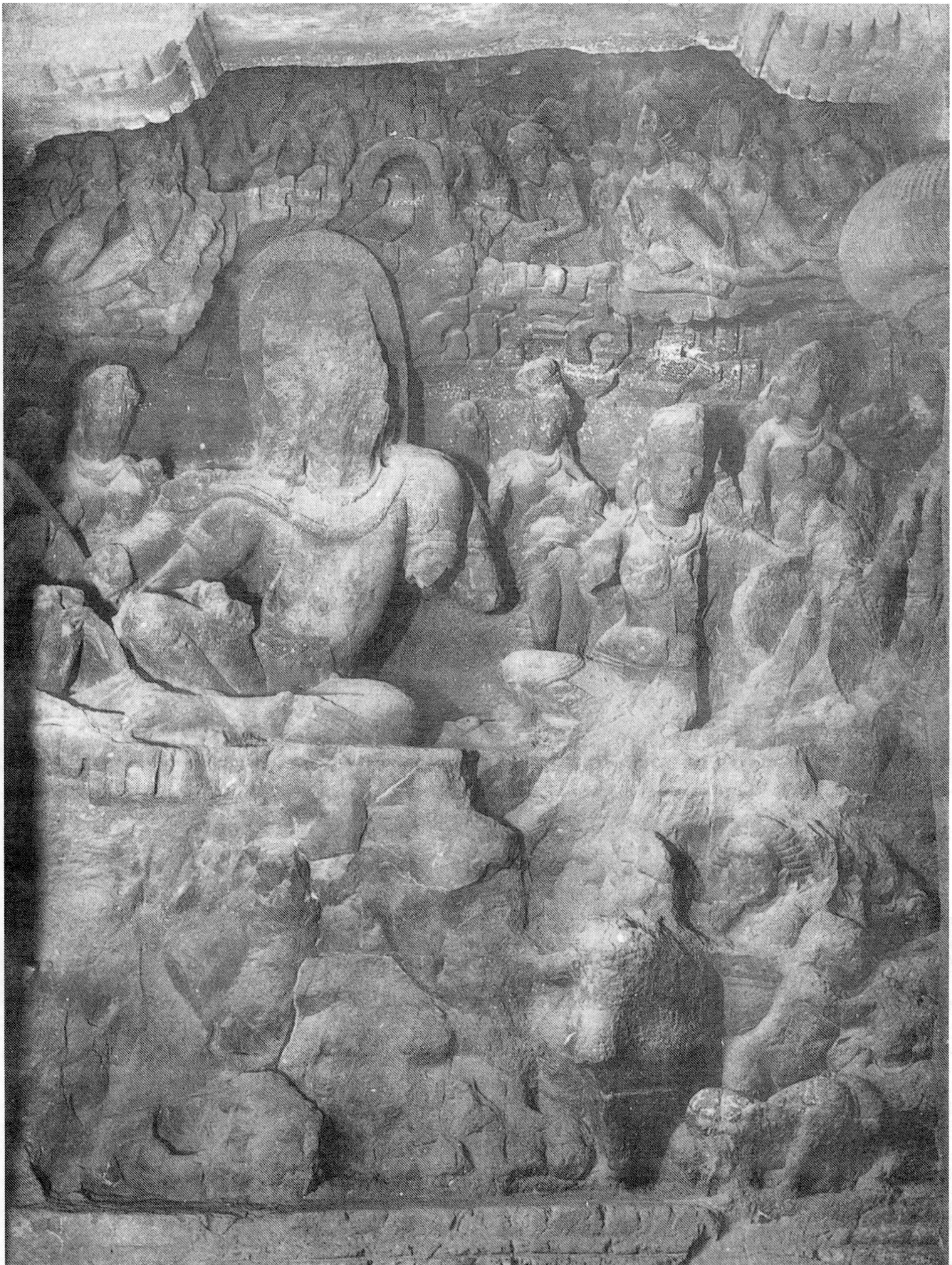

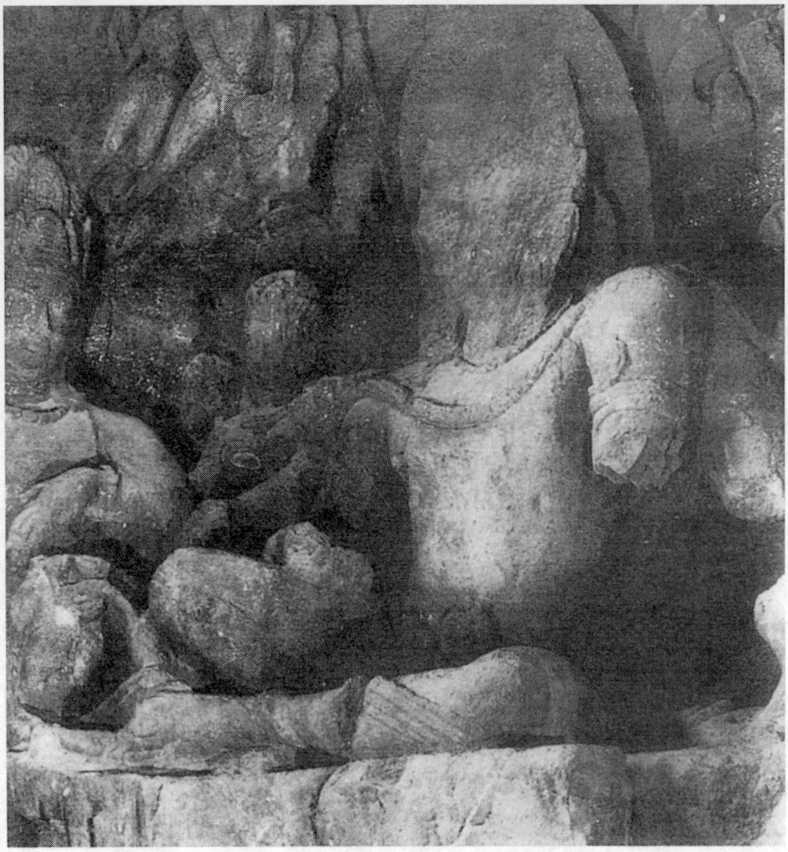

PL. 27. Umamaheshvara—the Gambling Scene, Shiva seated, accompanied by a female attendant and a doorkeeper standing in the east corner, with flying figures and Bhringi.

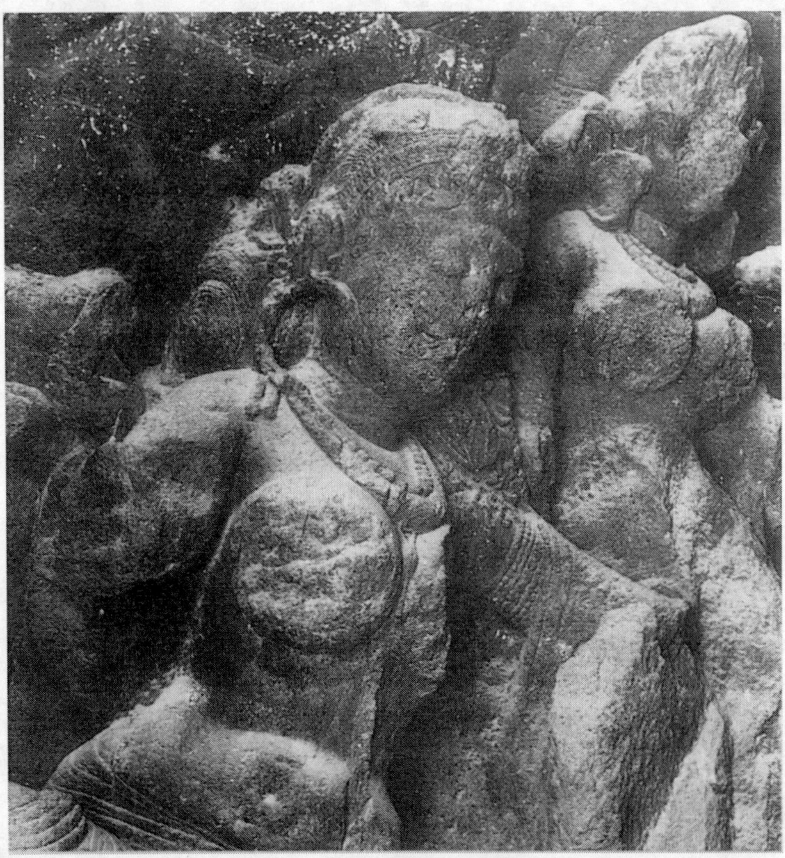

PL. 28. Umamaheshvara—the Gambling Scene, Parvati and attendants.

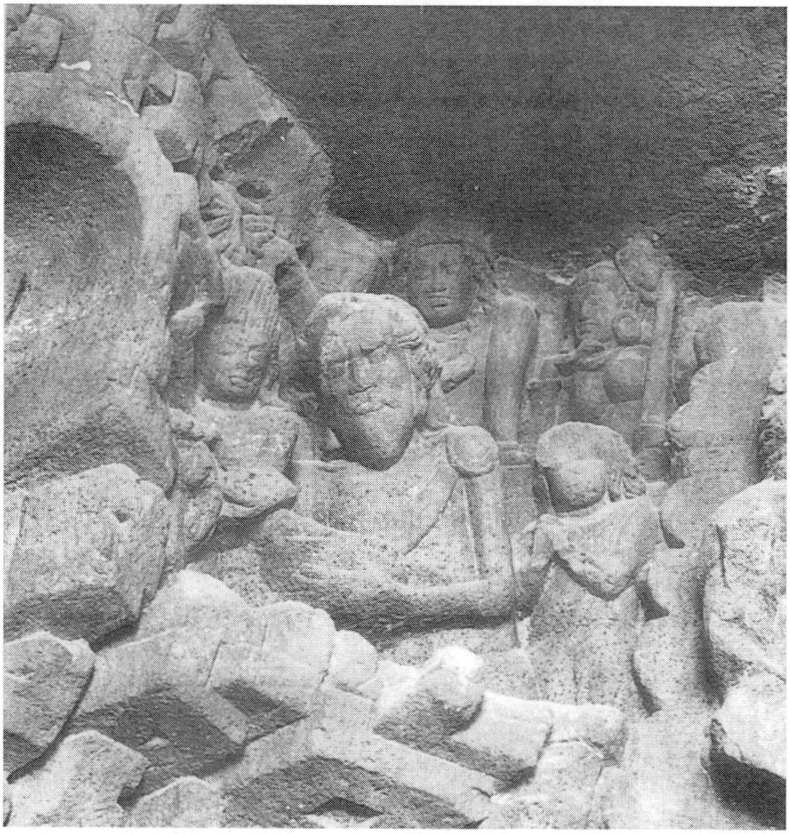

PL. 29. Umamaheshvara—the Gambling Scene, the worshipers above Shiva and Parvati on Mt. Kailasa.

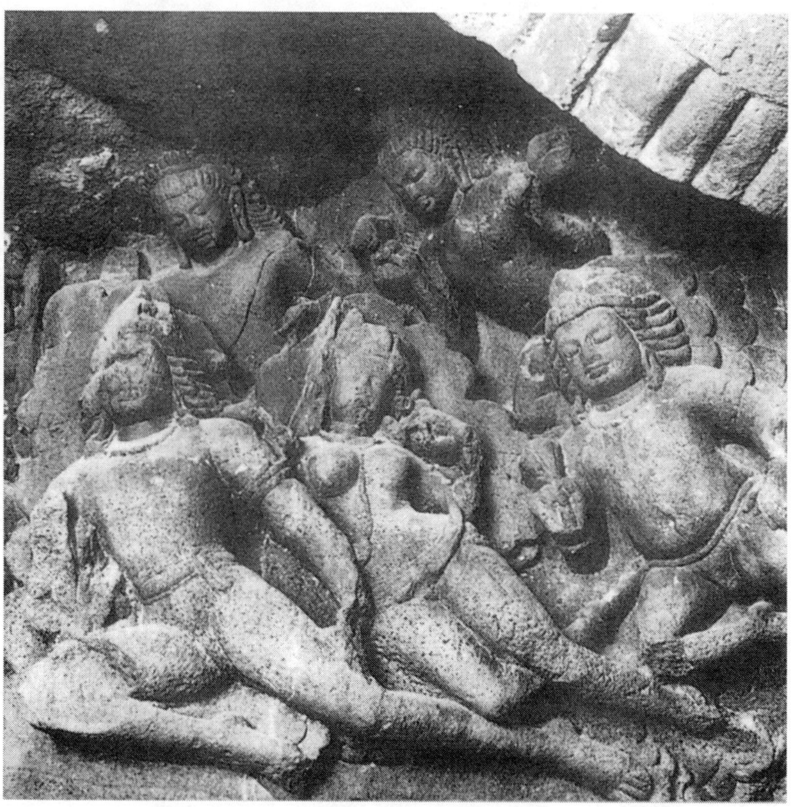

PL. 30. Umamaheshvara—the Gambling Scene, flying figures.

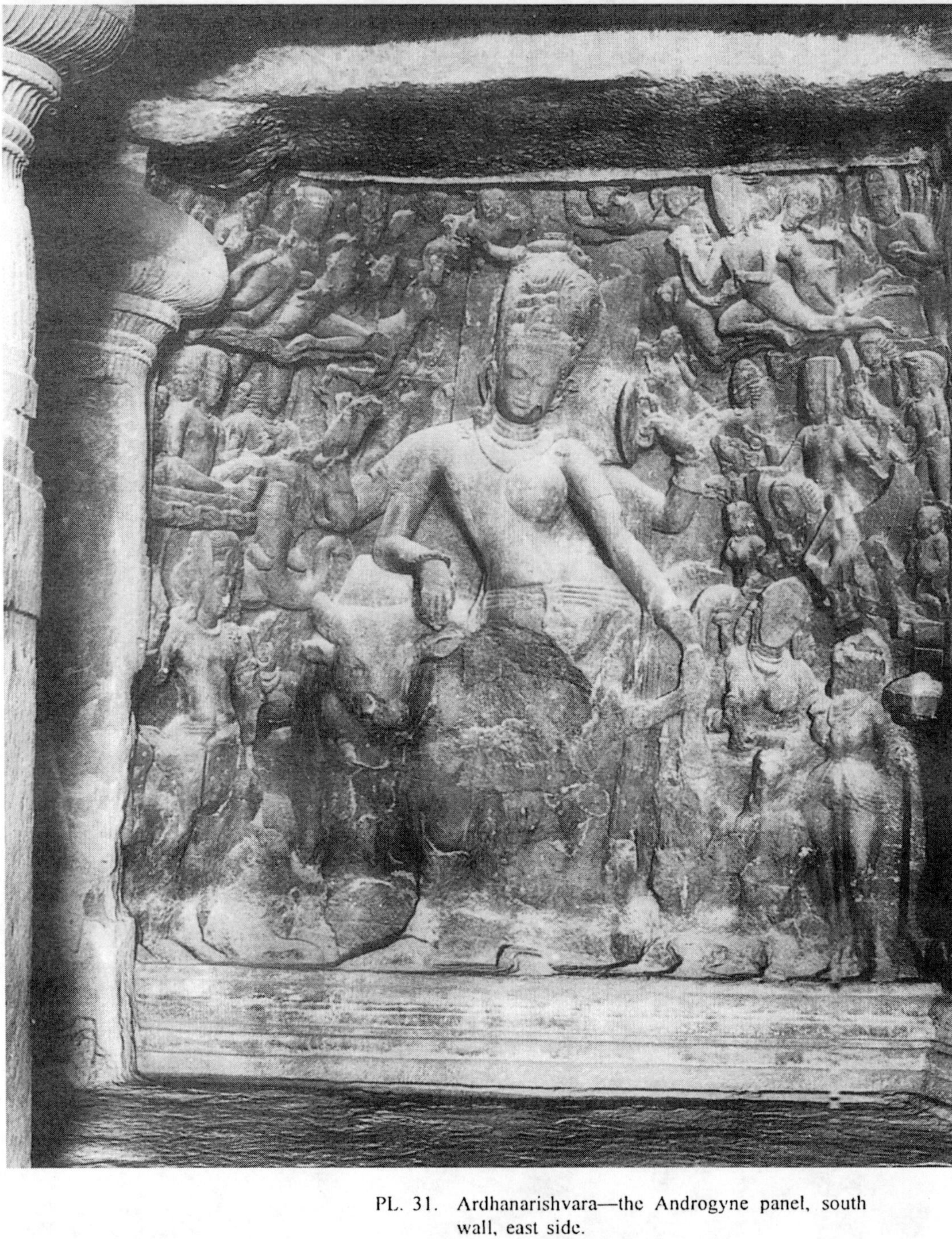

PL. 31. Ardhanarishvara—the Androgyne panel, south wall, east side.

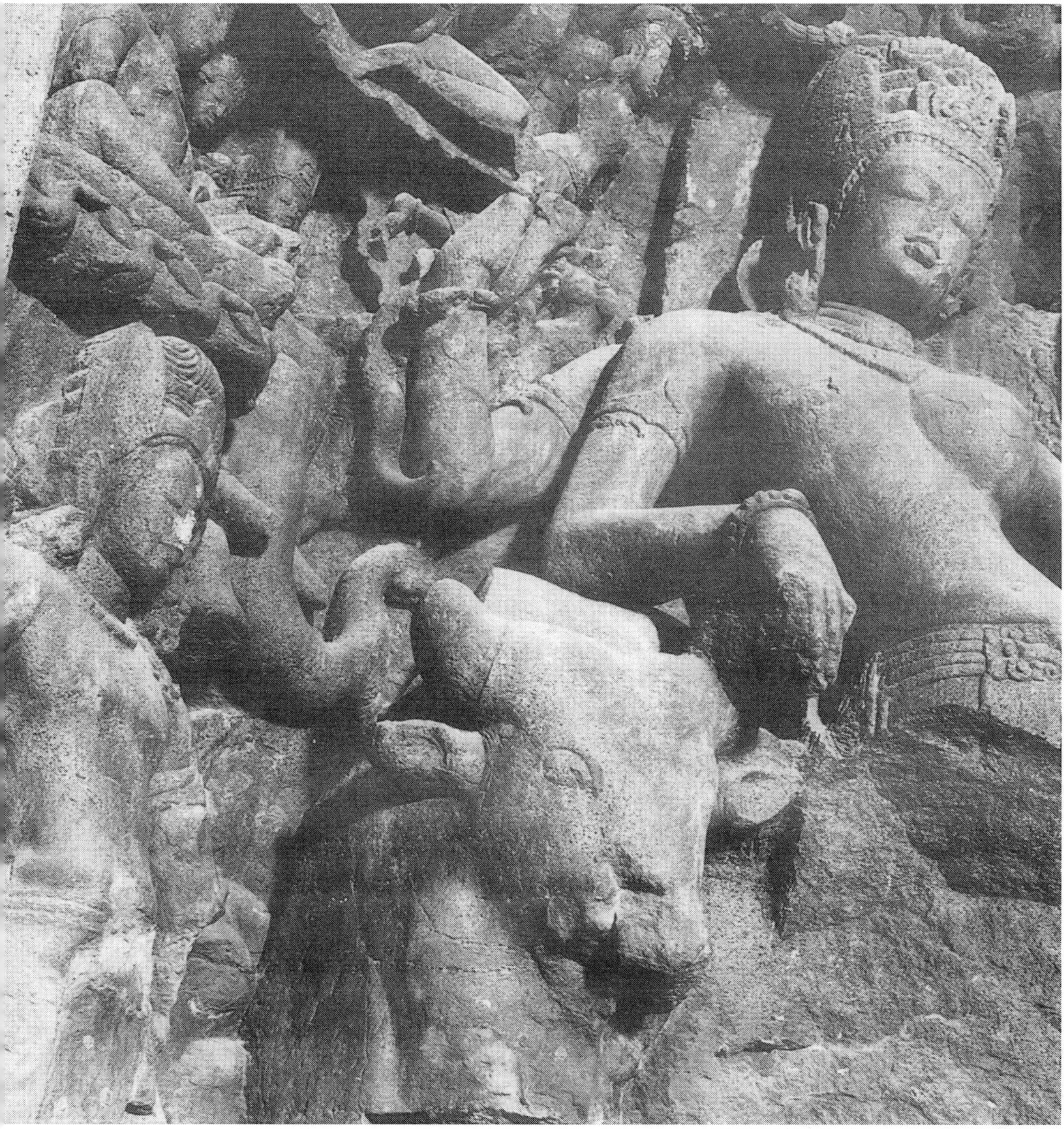

PL. 32. Ardhanarishvara—the Androgyne, a view from a seat at the doorstep of the adjacent cell, showing the newly developed understanding of three dimensional form.

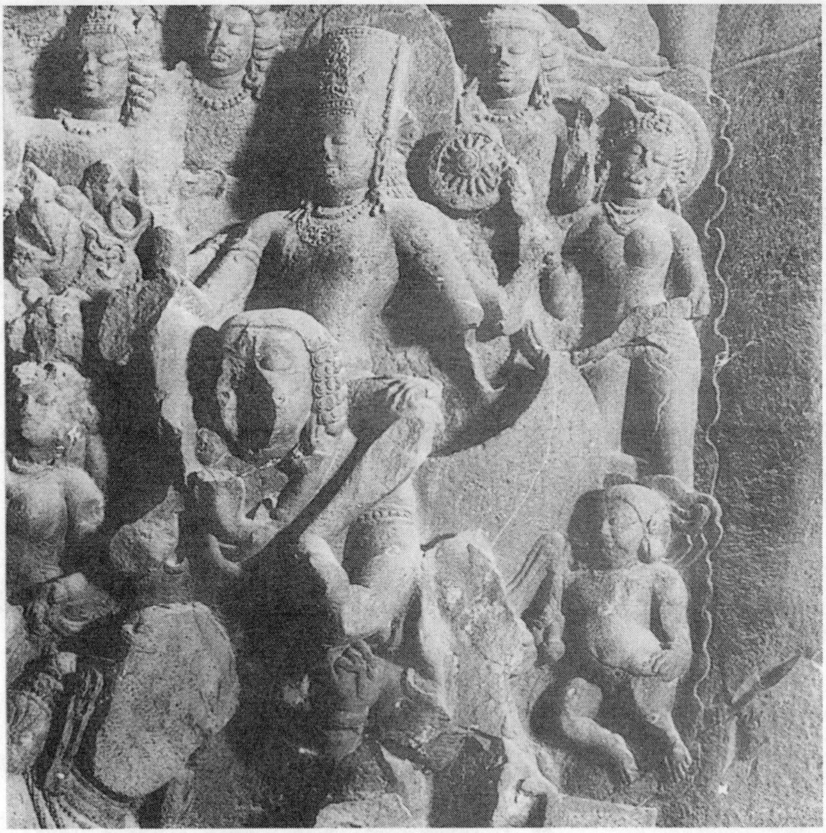

PL. 33. Ardhanarishvara—the Androgyne, Varuna on the *makara* and Vishnu on Garuda surrounded by a circle of attendants.

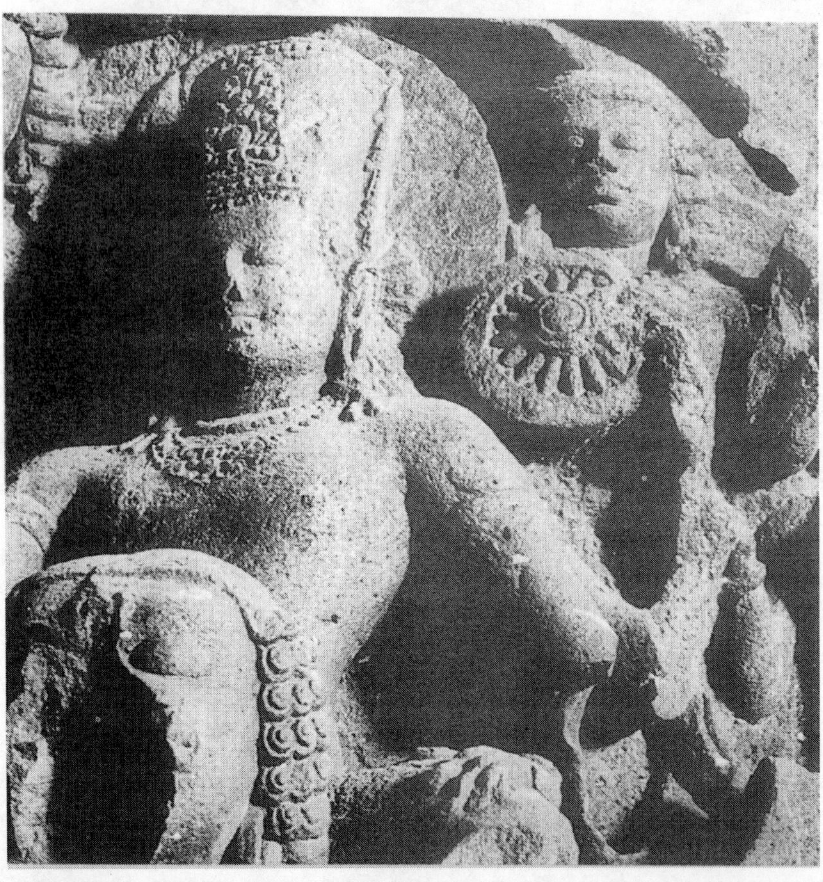

PL. 34. Ardhanarishvara—the Androgyne, Vishnu on Garuda.

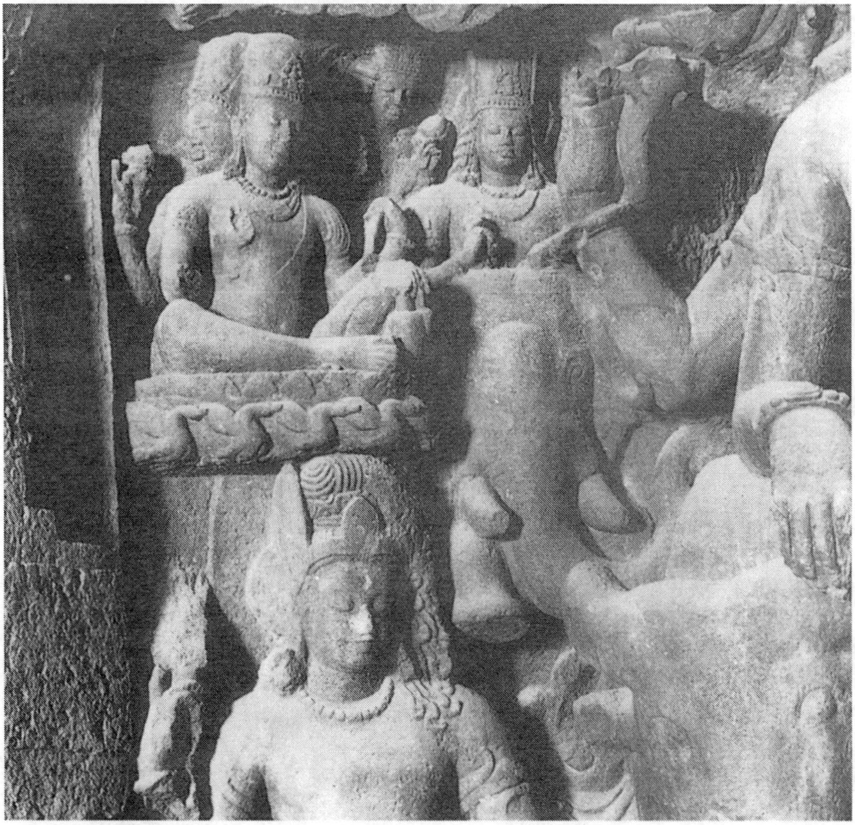

PL. 35. Ardhanarishvara—the Androgyne, Brahma on his seat of swans, Indra on the elephant; below; the upper portion of Kartikeya.

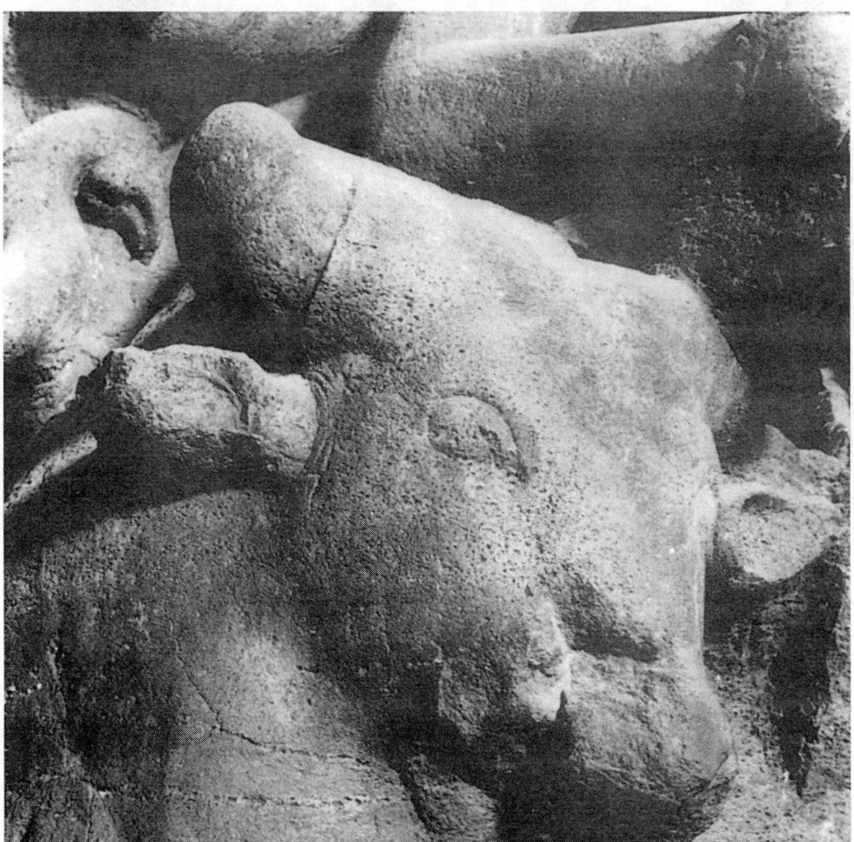

PL. 36. Ardhanarishvara—the Androgyne, Nandi.

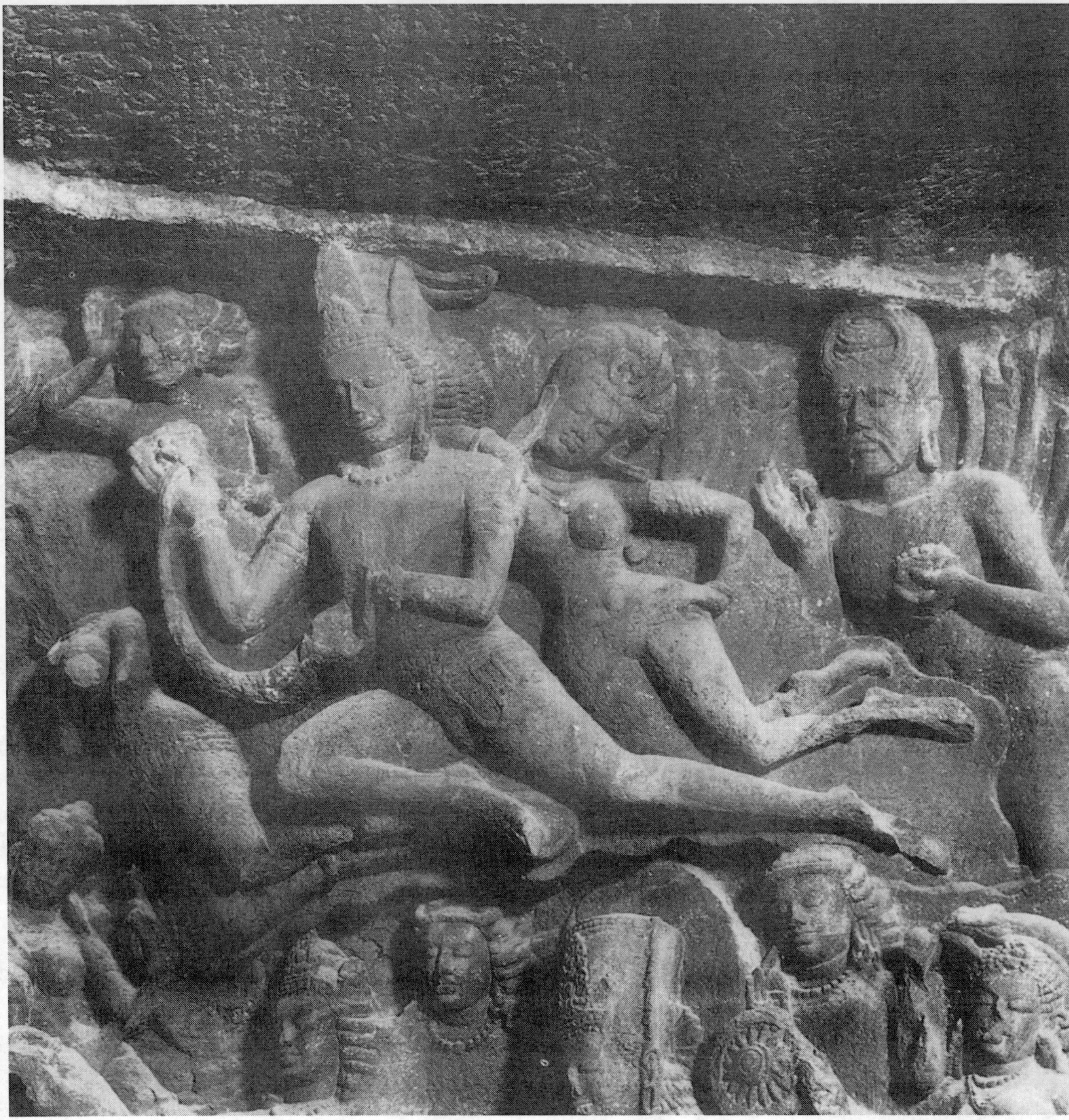

PL. 37. Ardhanarishvara—the Androgyne, flying figures.

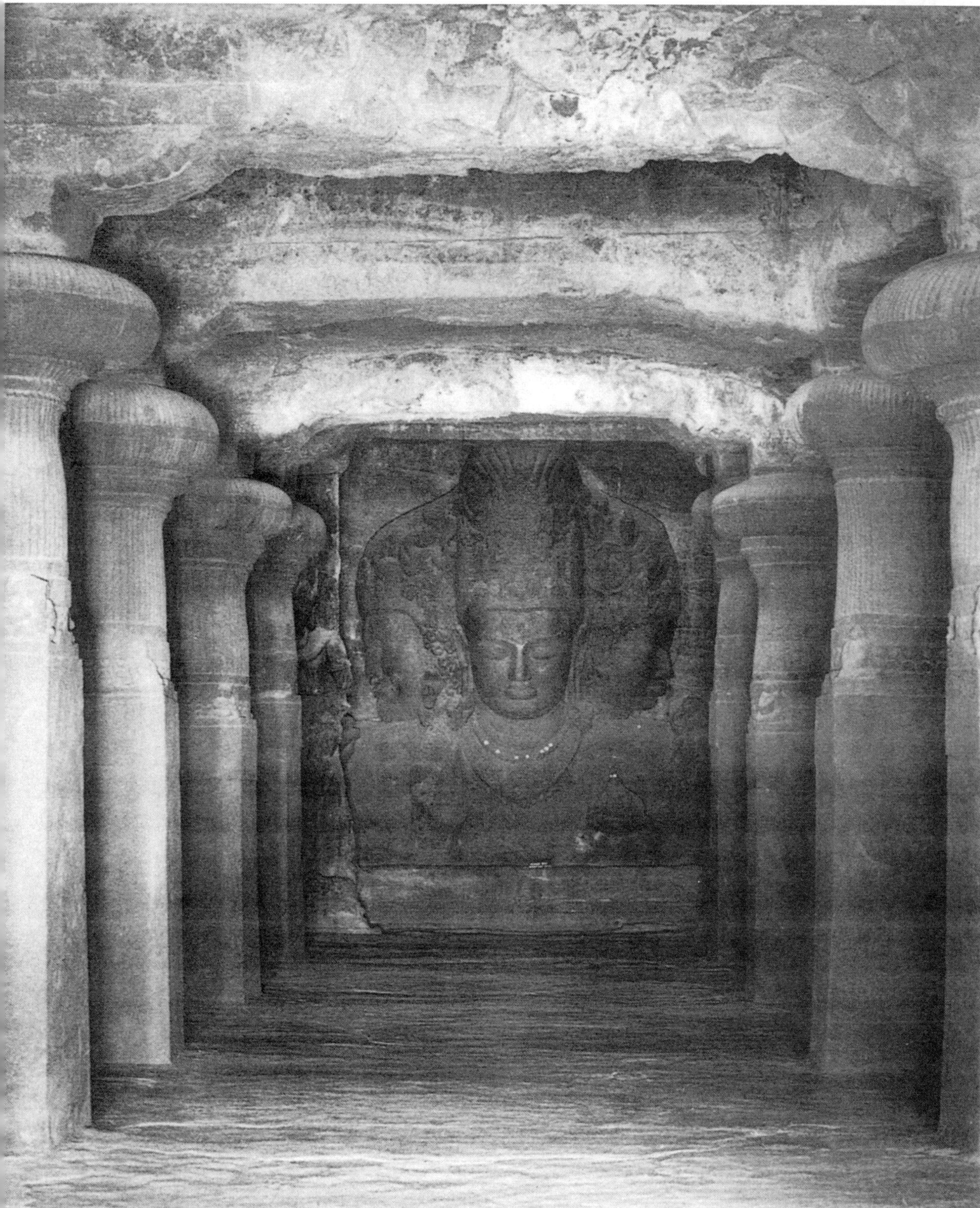

PL. 38. Sadashiva—Eternal Shiva panel, south wall, with row of columns.

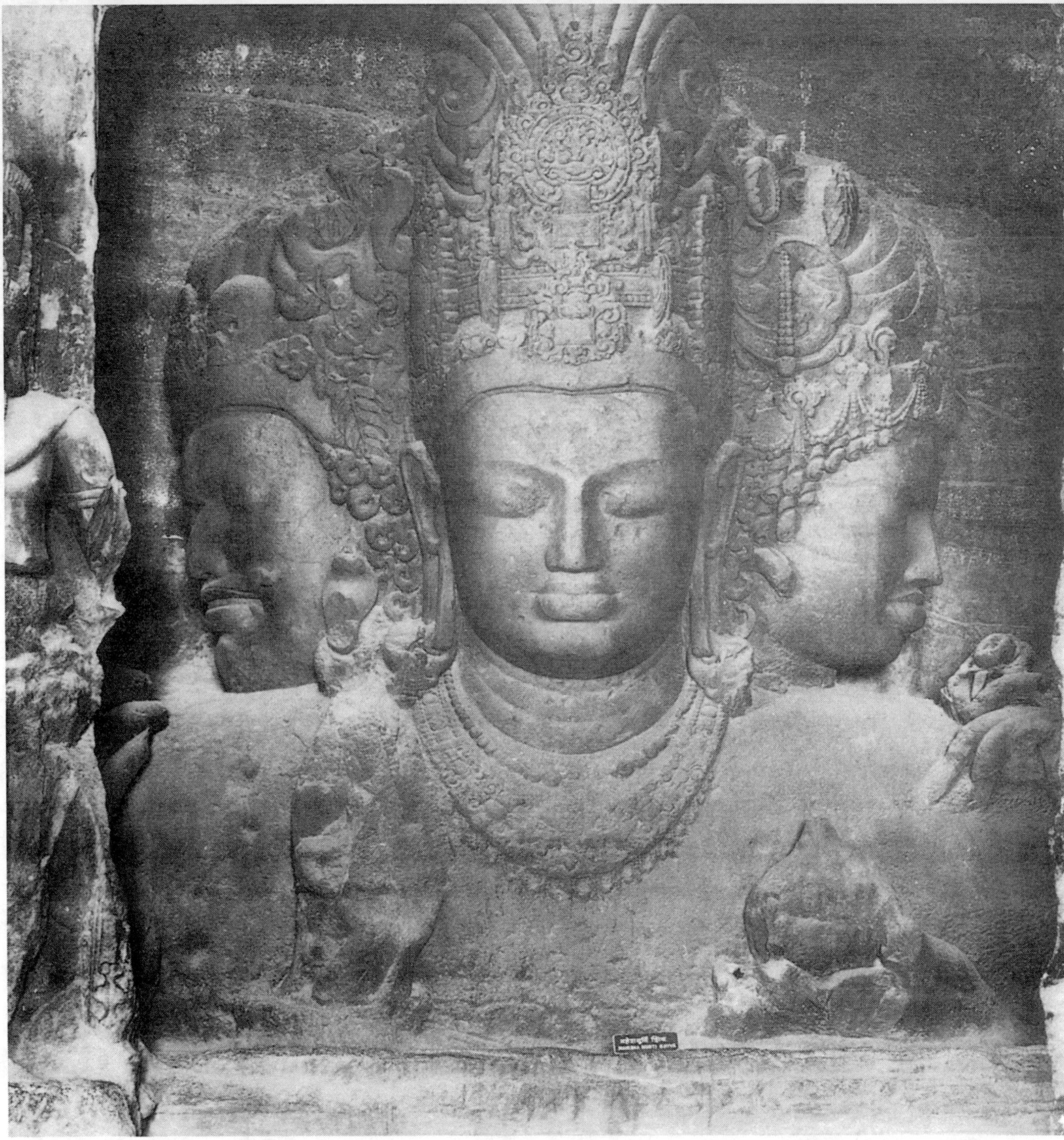

PL. 39. Sadashiva—Eternal Shiva, south wall, central panel.

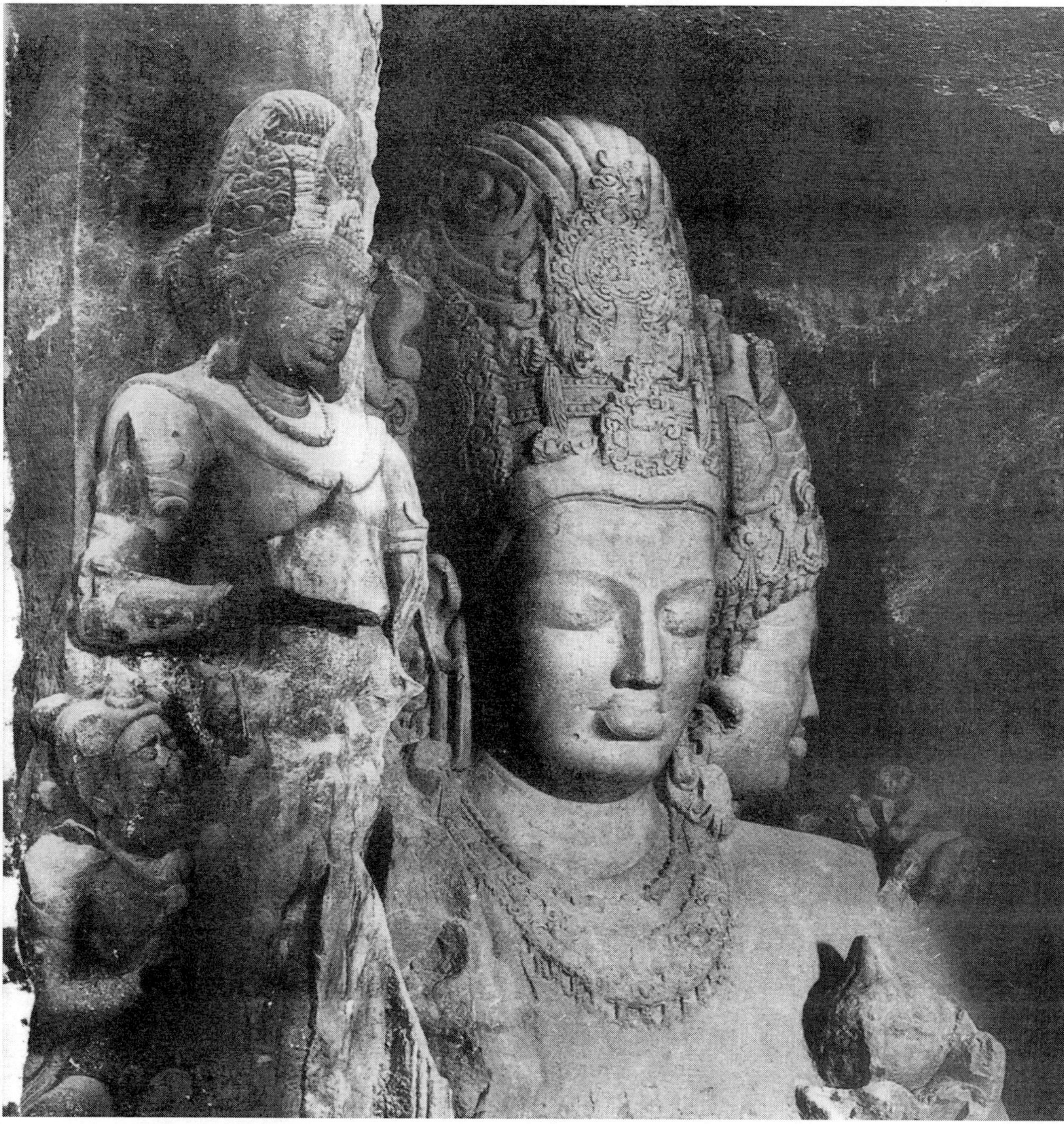

PL. 40. Sadashiva—Eternal Shiva, Tatpurusha and Vamadeva with doorkeeper and dwarf to the right.

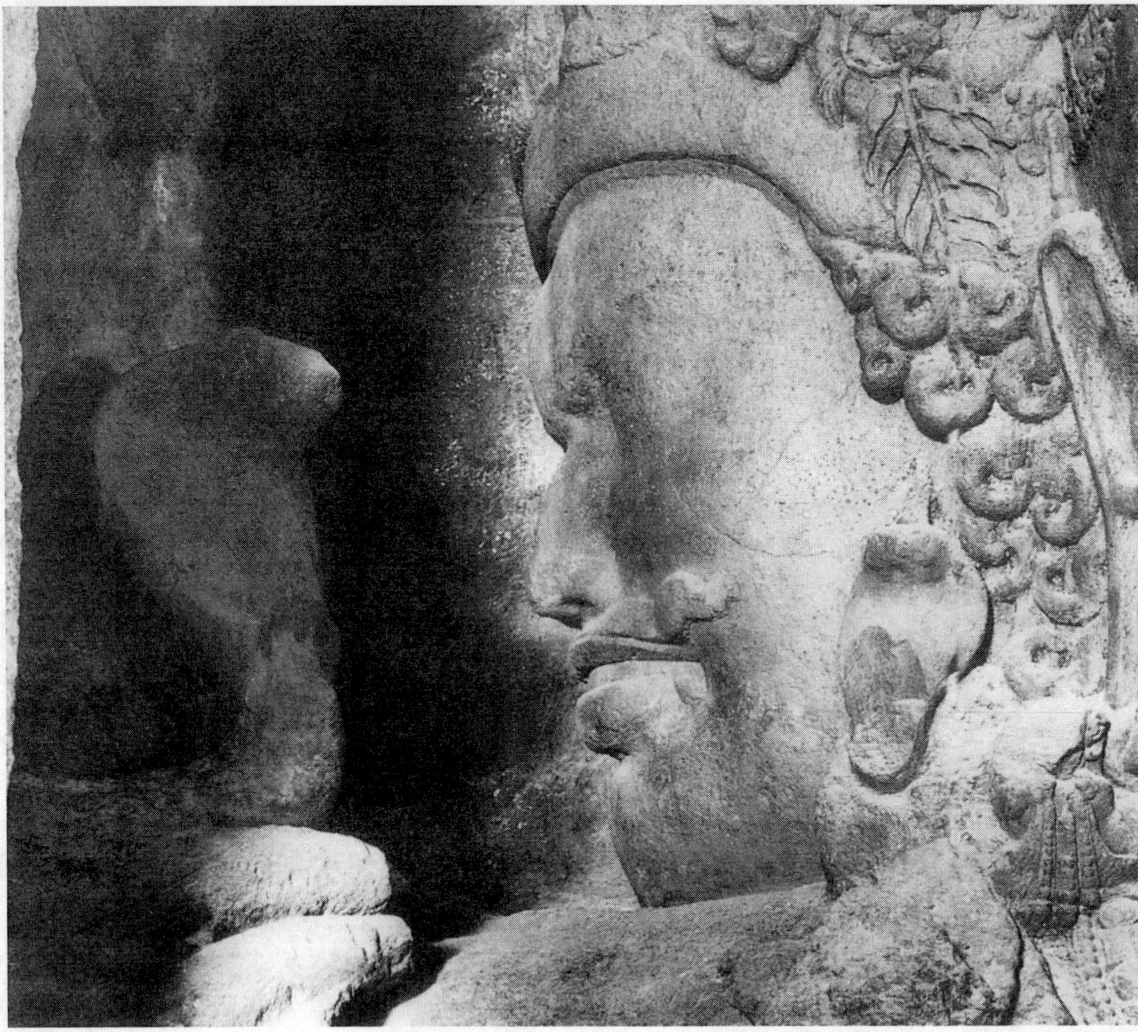

PL. 41. Sadashiva—Eternal Shiva, Aghora with cobra.

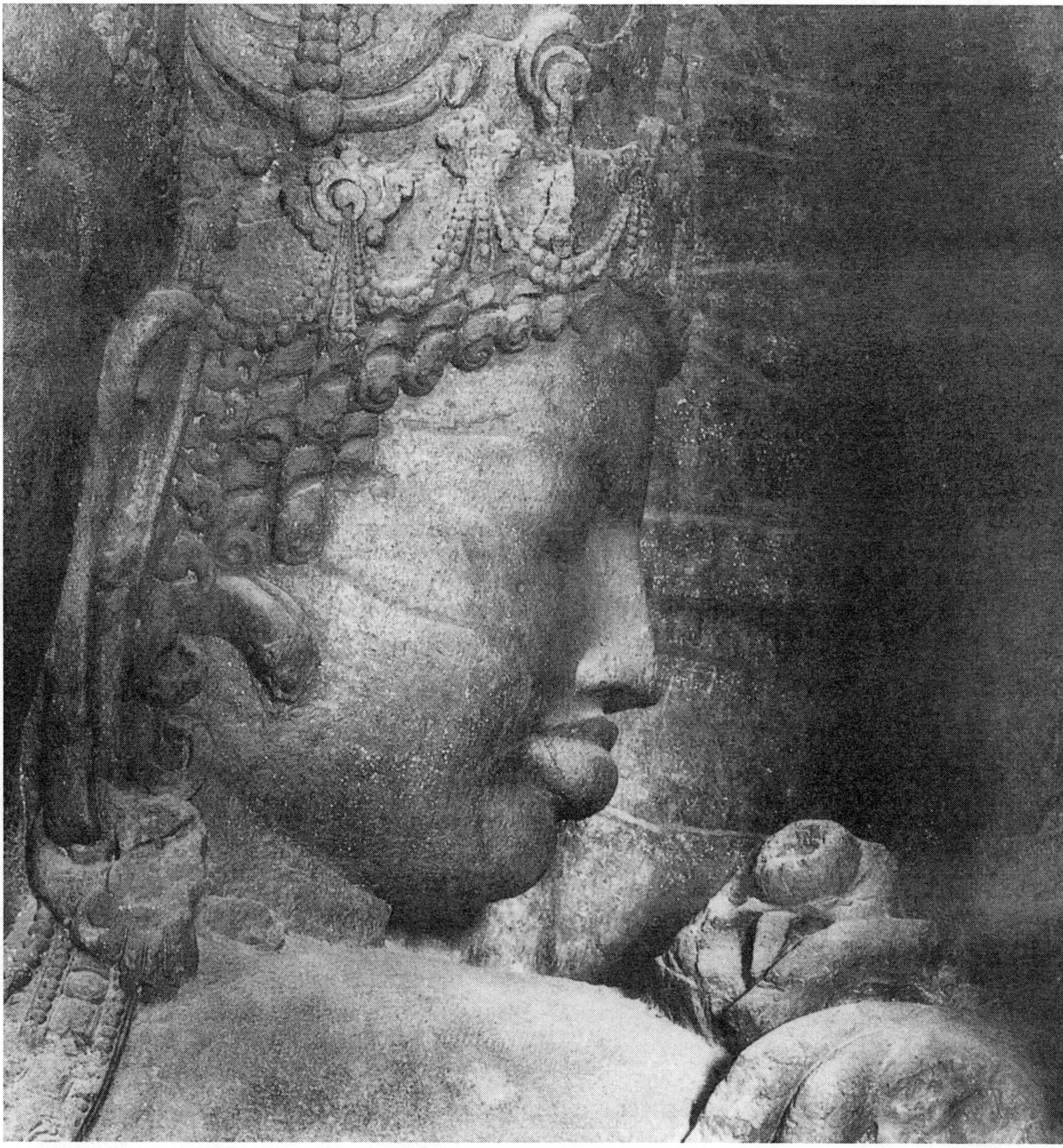

PL. 42. Sadashiva—Eternal Shiva, Vamadeva with lotus.

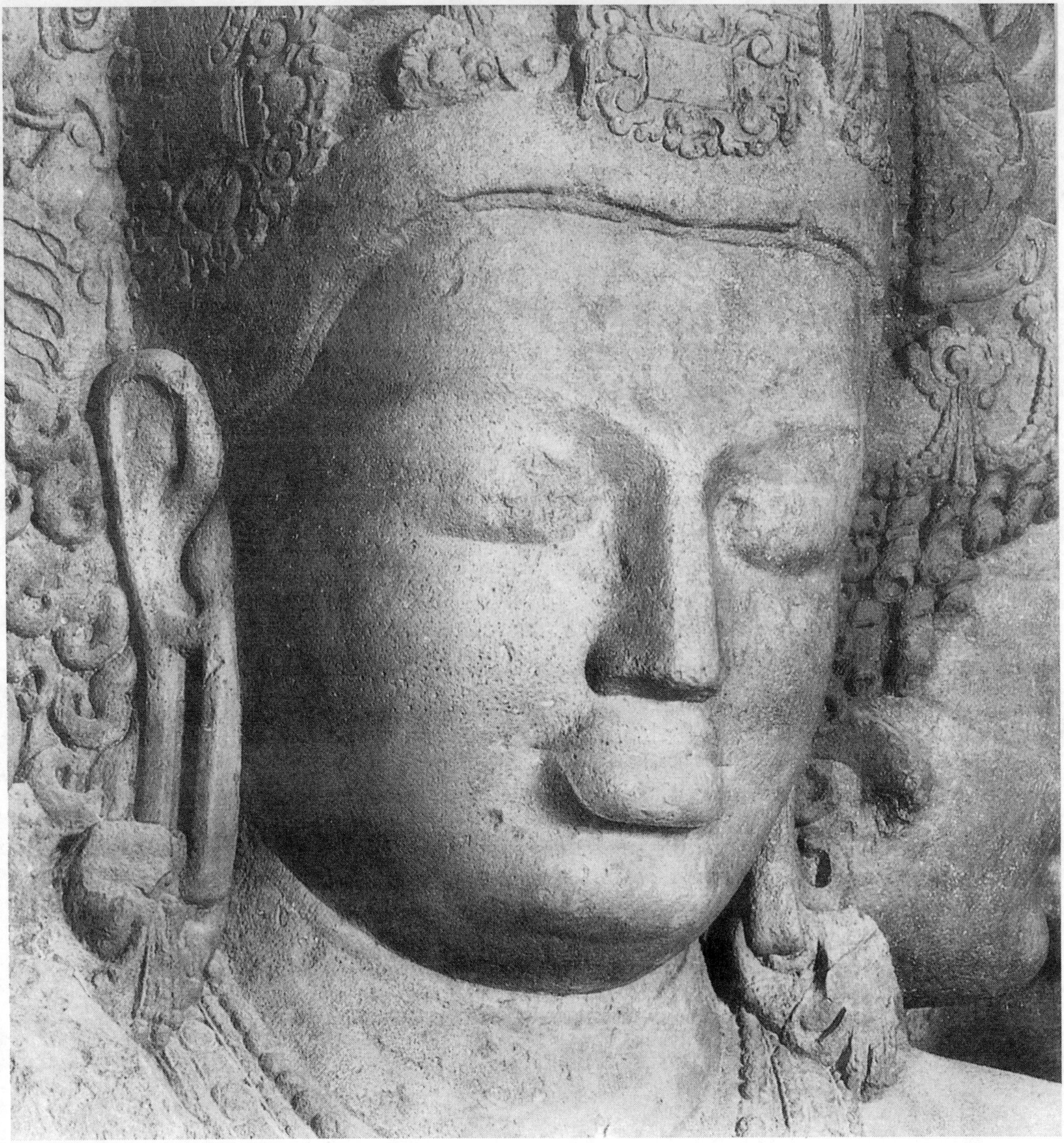

PL. 43. Sadashiva—Eternal Shiva, Tatpurusha.

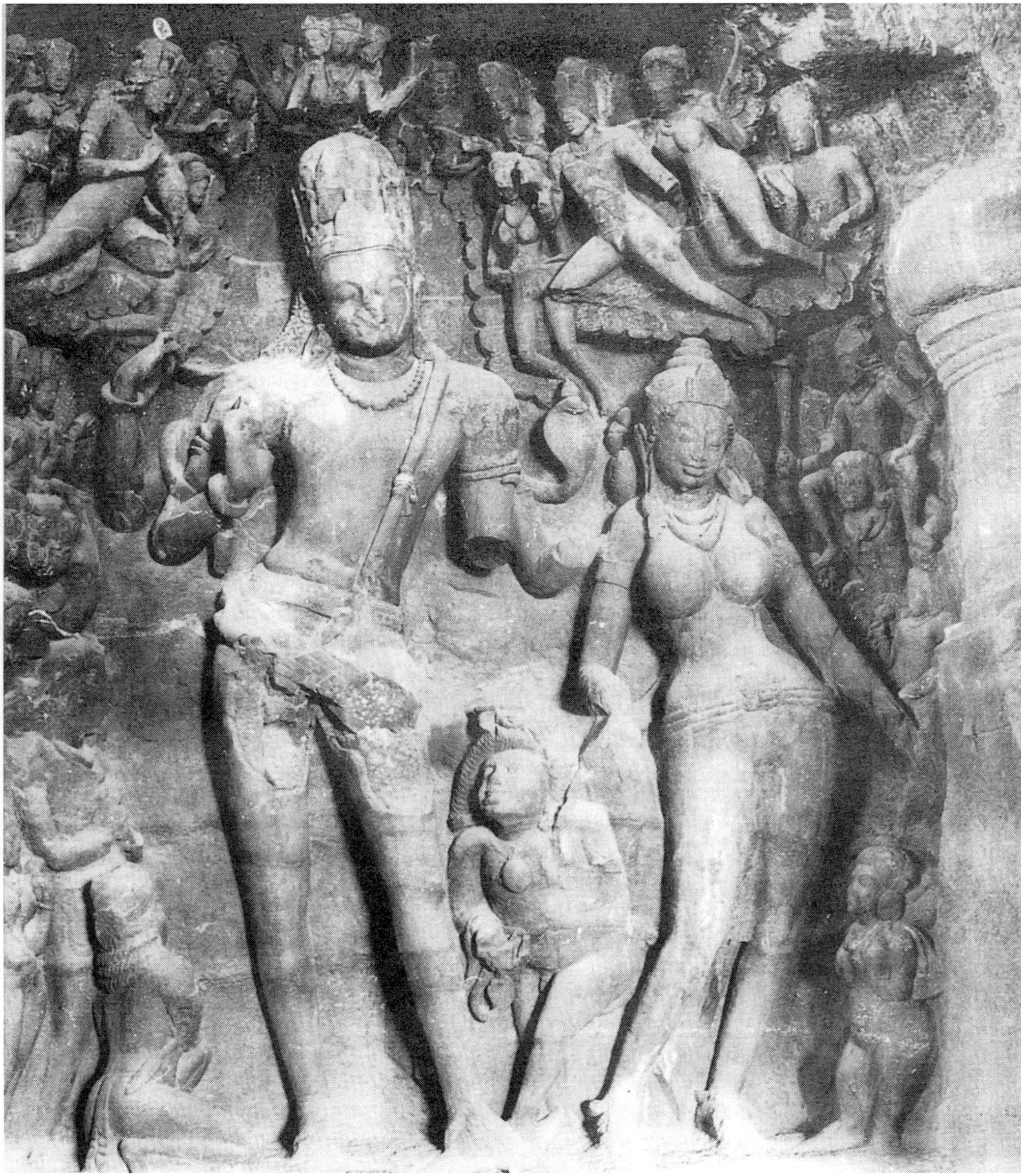

PL. 44. Gangadhara—(Descent of the) Ganges panel, south wall, west side.

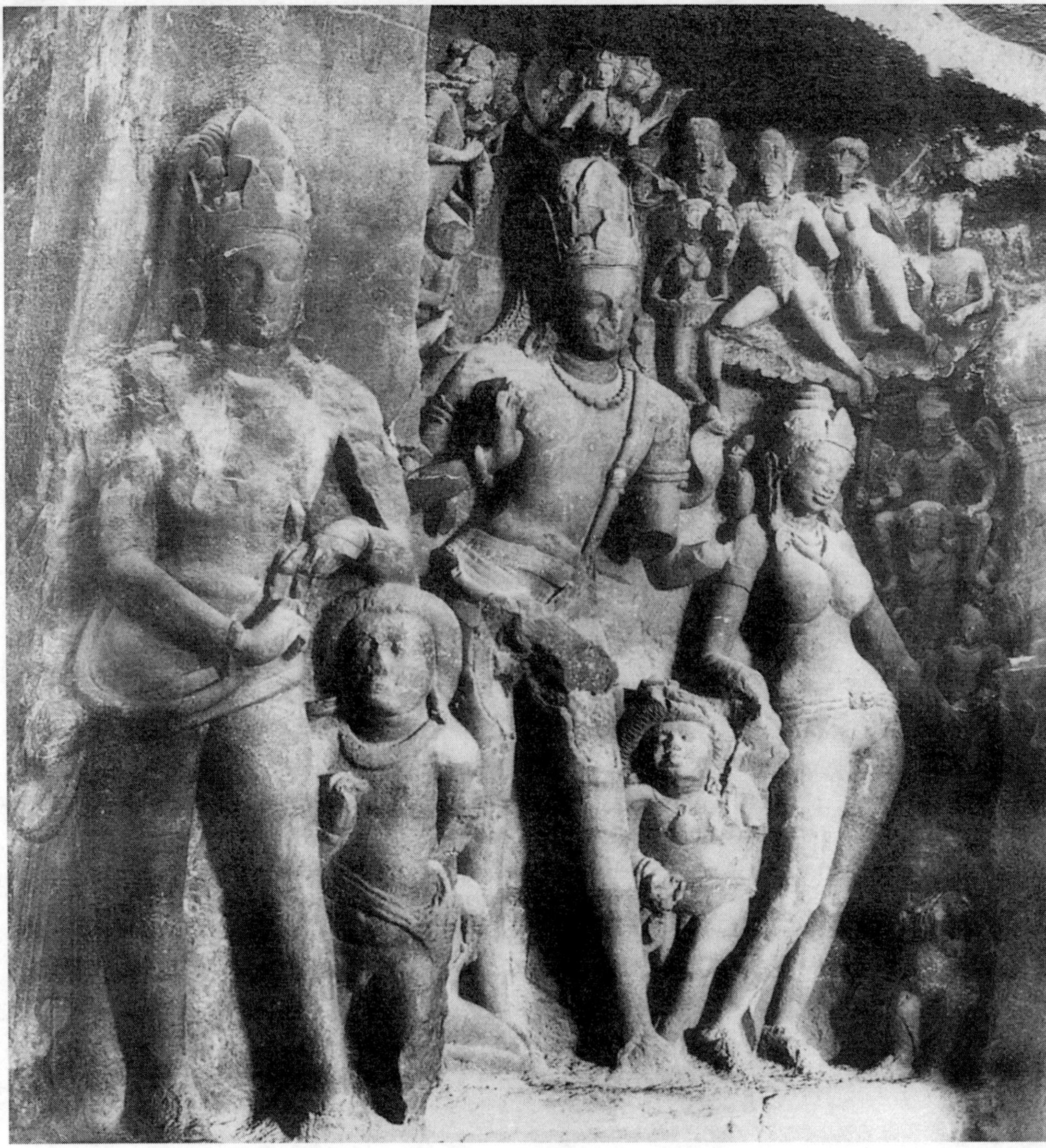

PL. 45. Gangadhara—(Descent of the) Ganges, with doorkeeper and dwarf.

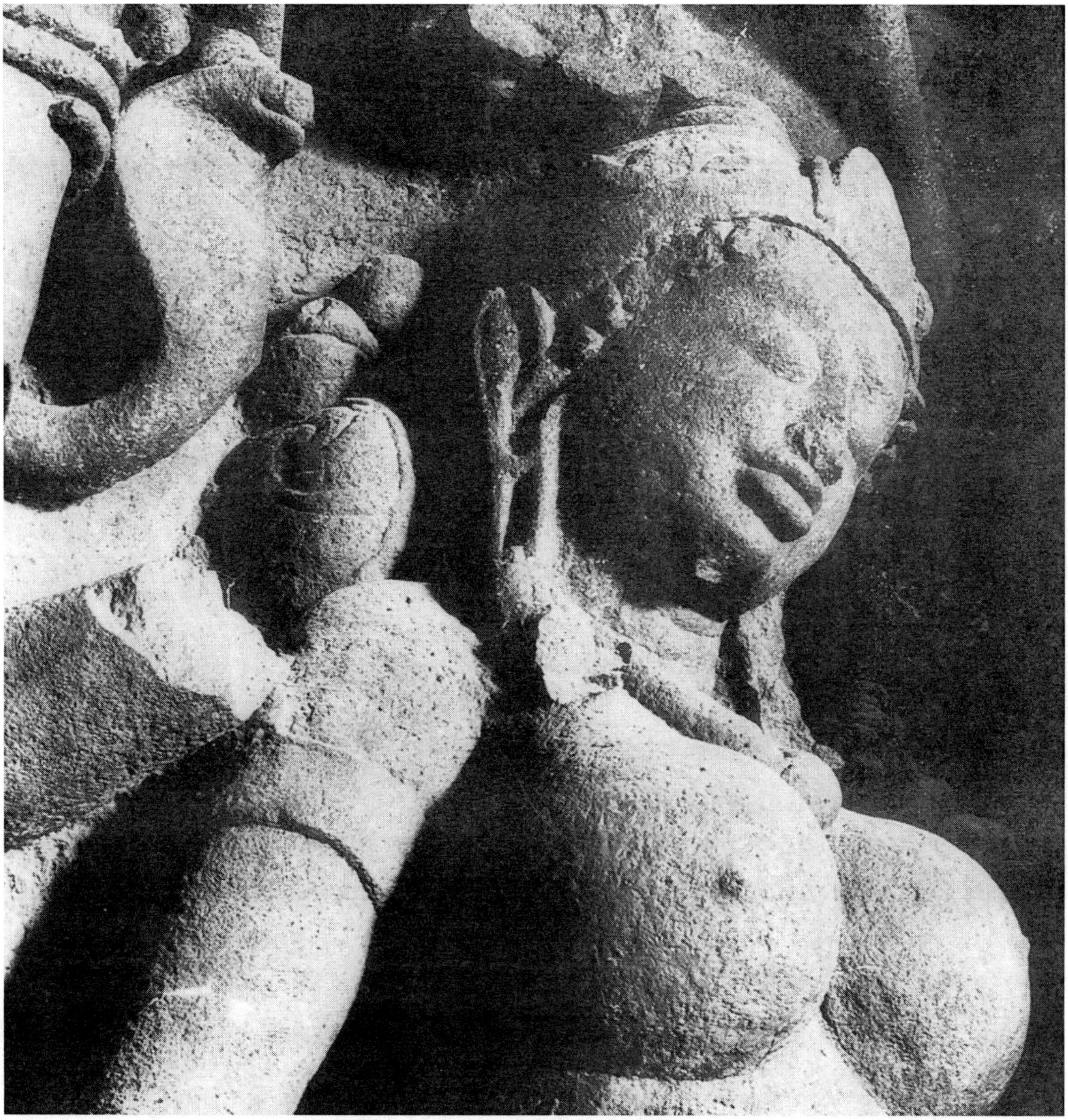

PL. 46. Gangadhara—(Descent of the) Ganges, Parvati, detail.

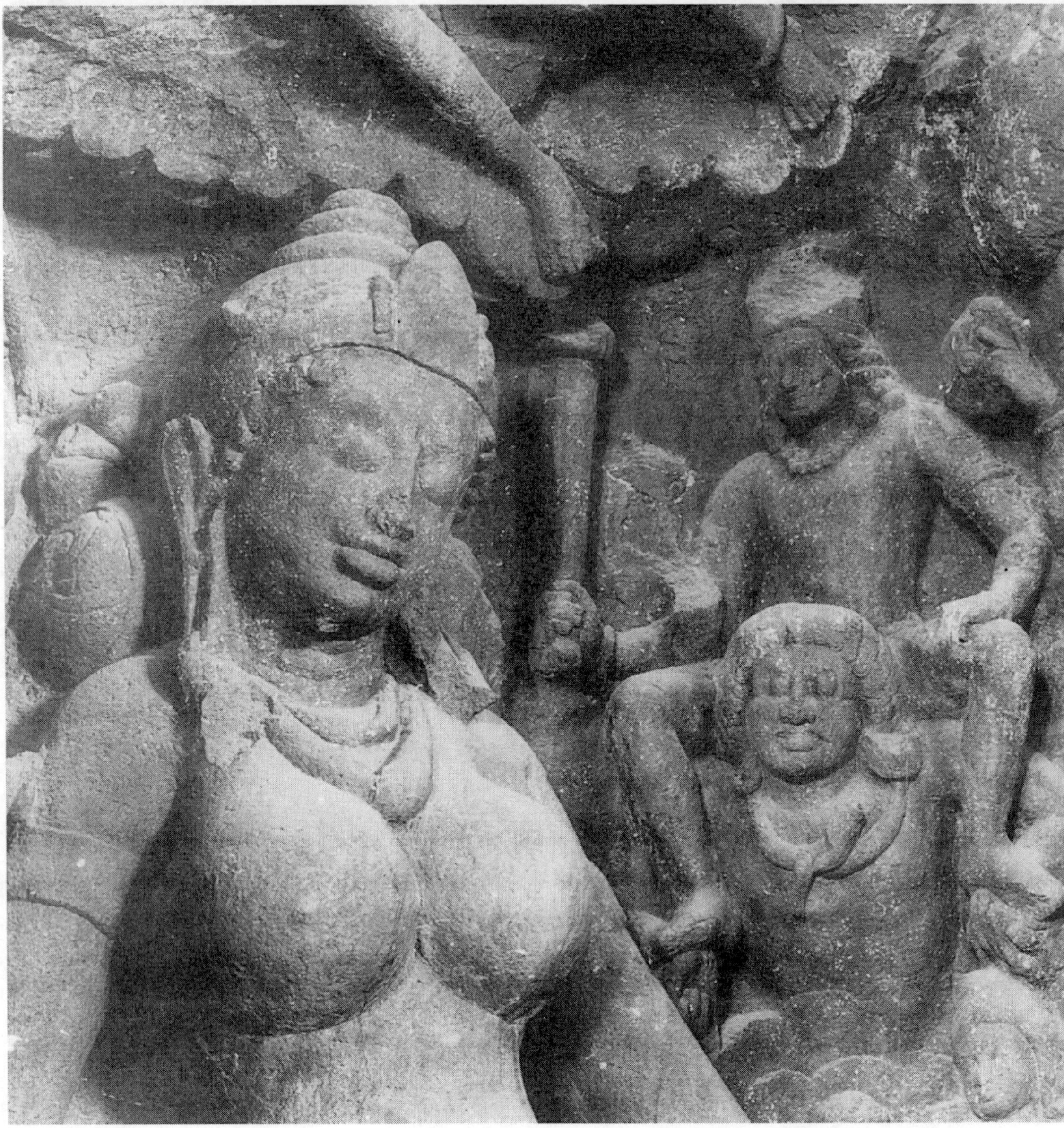

PL. 47. Gangadhara—(Descent of the) Ganges, Parvati, with Vishnu on Garuda.

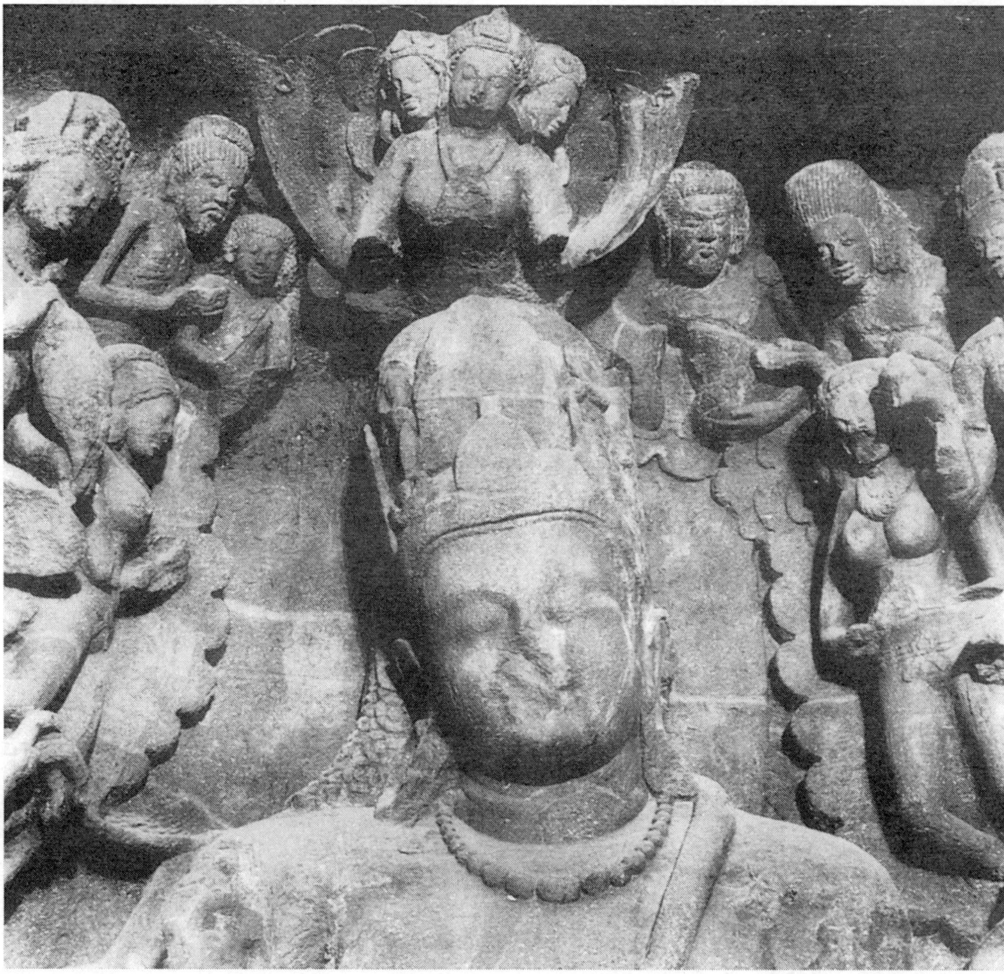

PL. 48. Gangadhara—(Descent of the) Ganges, head of Shiva surmounted by the Ganges river (which appears as a triple-headed goddess), and adoring worshipers.

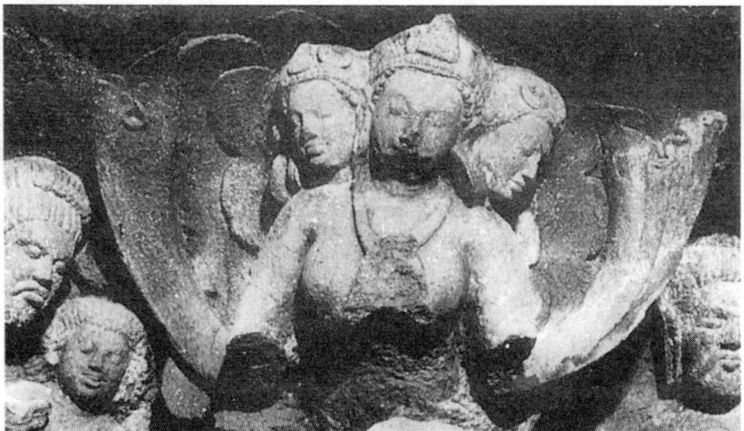

PL. 49. Detail PL. 48 three-headed Ganges river.

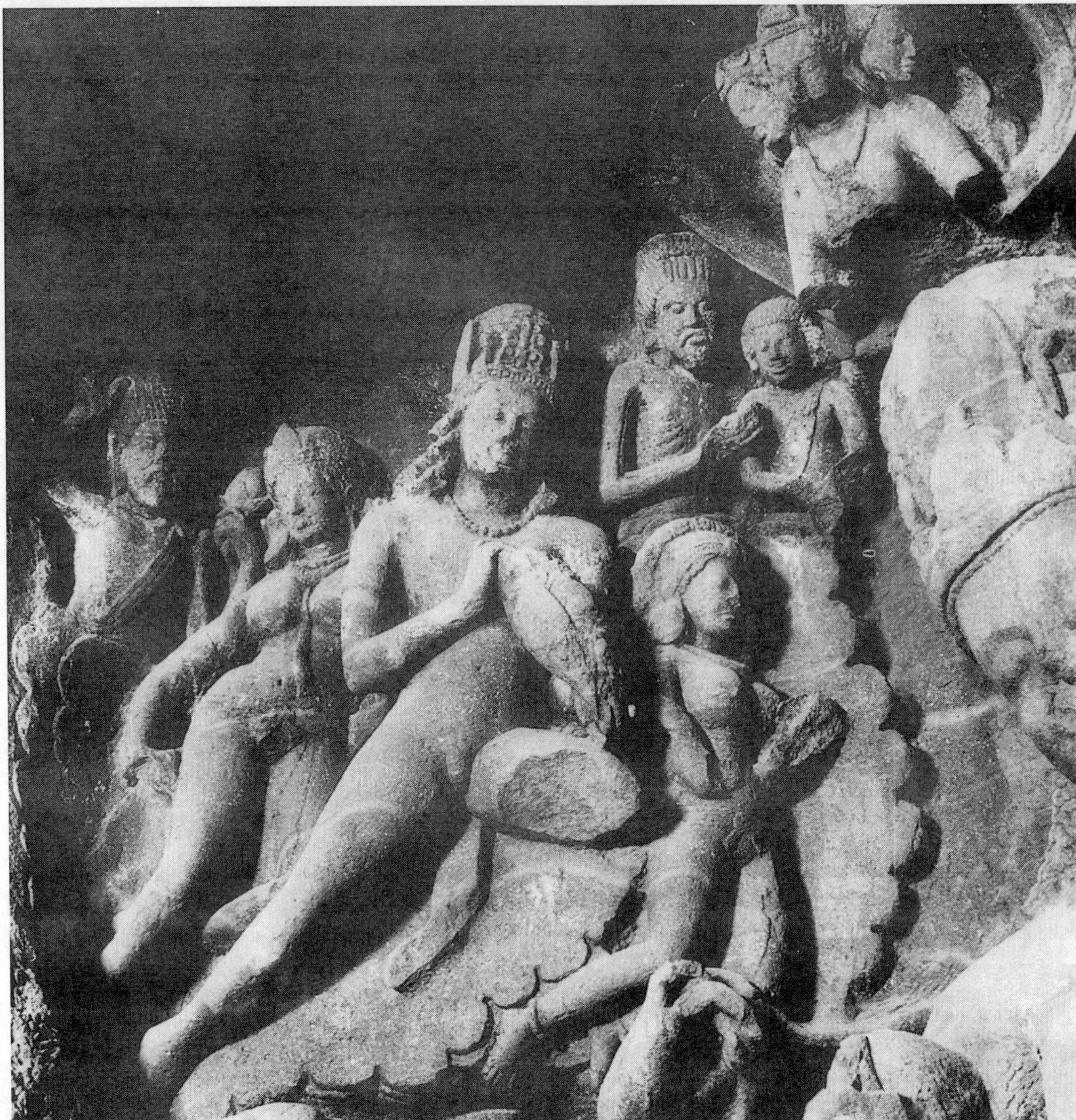

PL. 50. Gangadhara—(Descent of the) Ganges, flying figures and the three-headed Ganges river.

PL. 51. (Opposite) Kalyanasundara—Marriage (of Shiva and Parvati) panel, west veranda, south side.

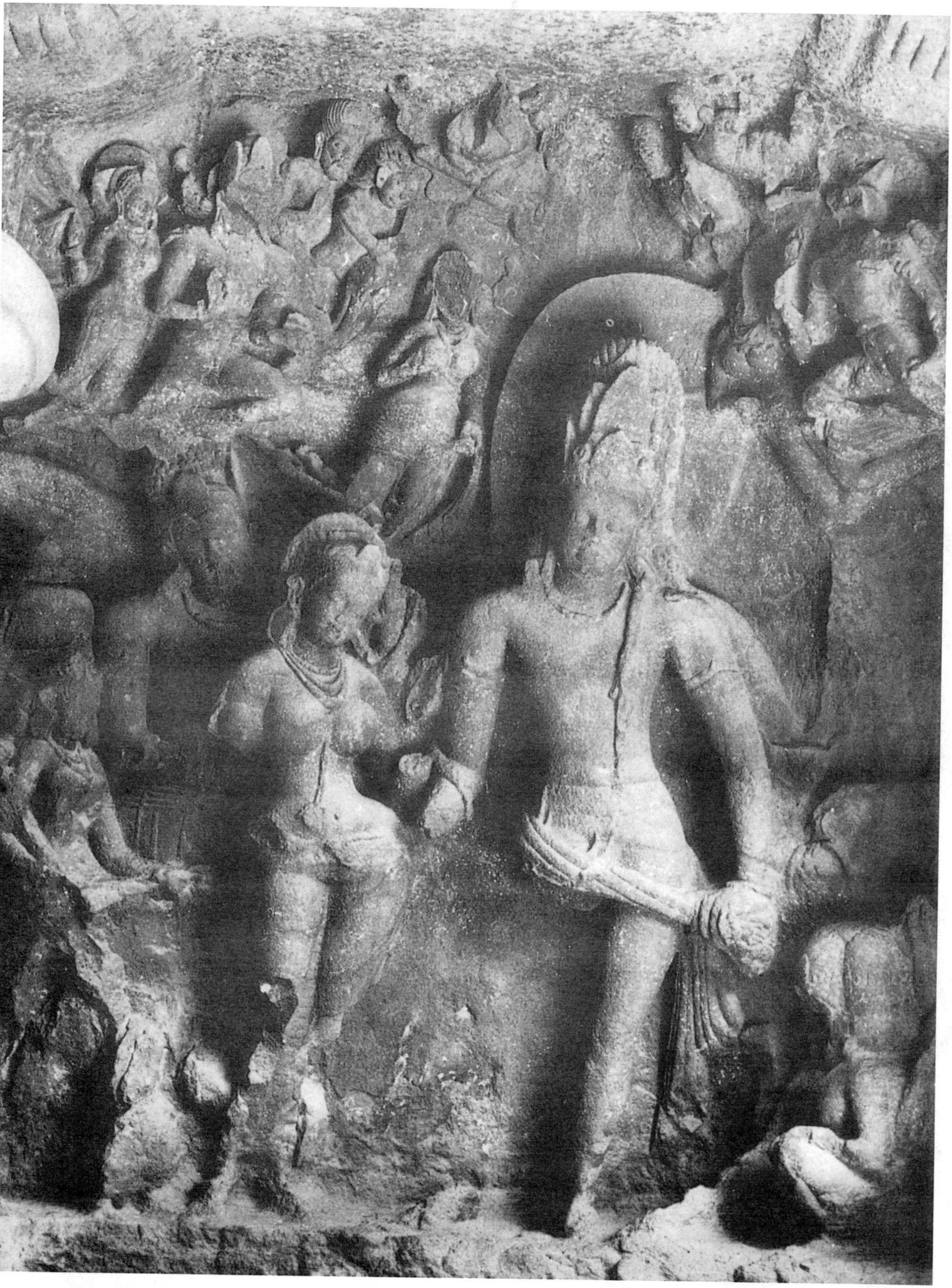

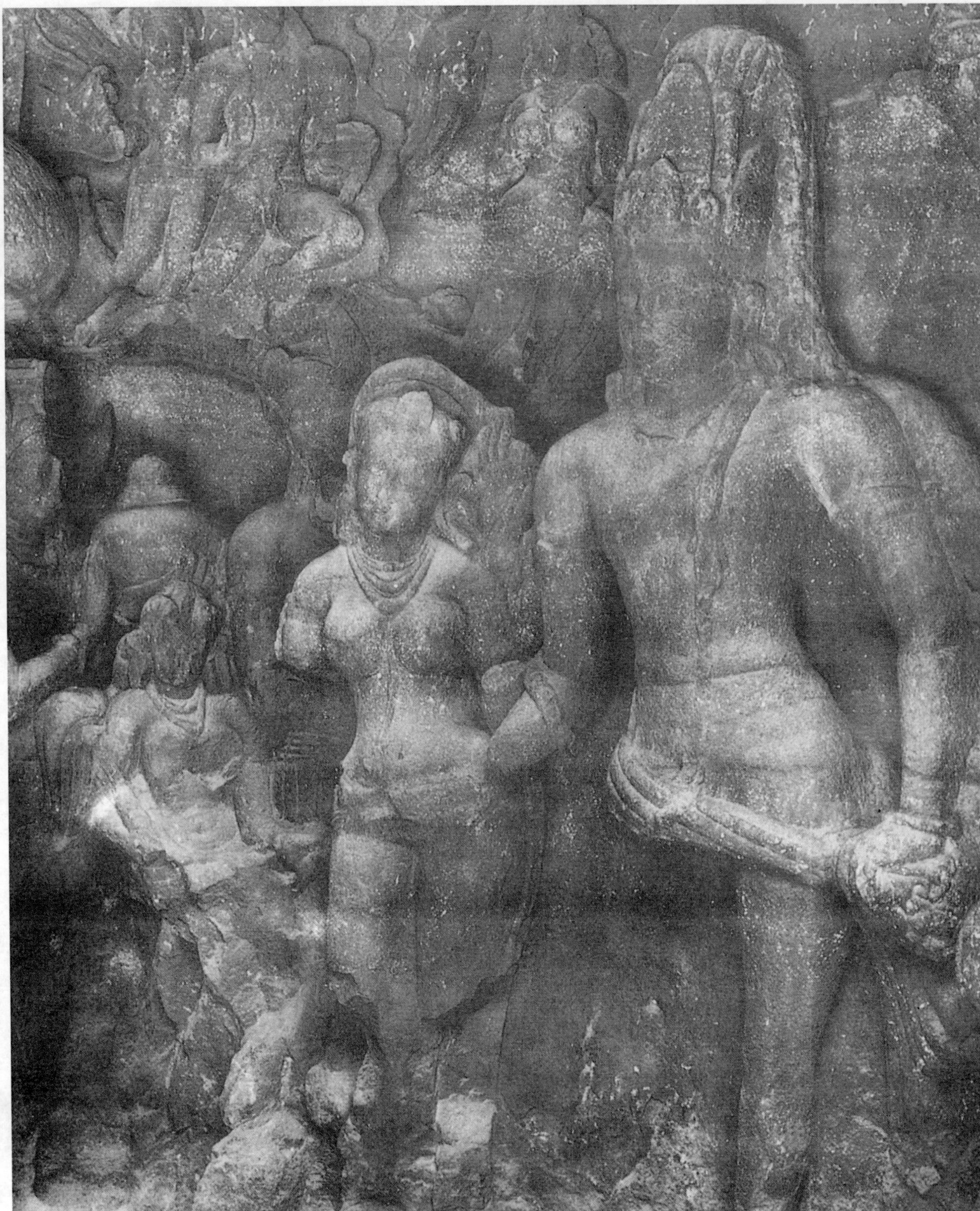

PL. 52. Kalyanasundara—Marriage (of Shiva and Parvati), a view from the west entrance.

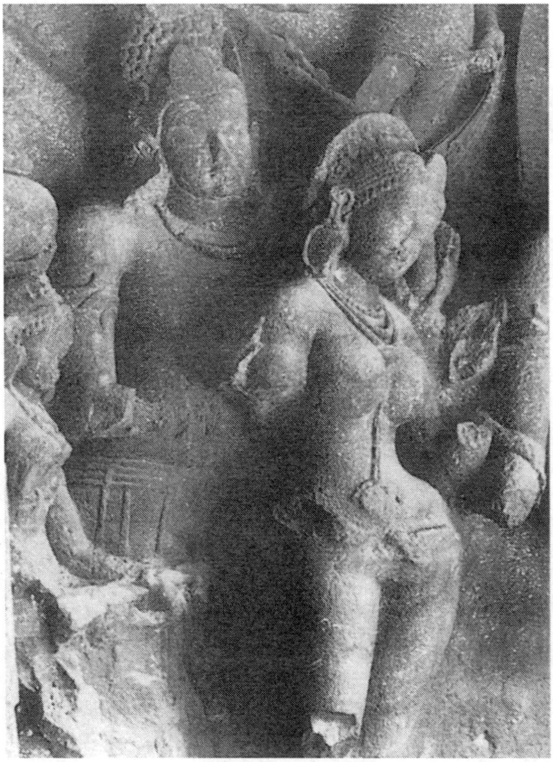

PL. 53. Kalyanasundara—Marriage (of Shiva and Parvati). Parvati and Himalaya

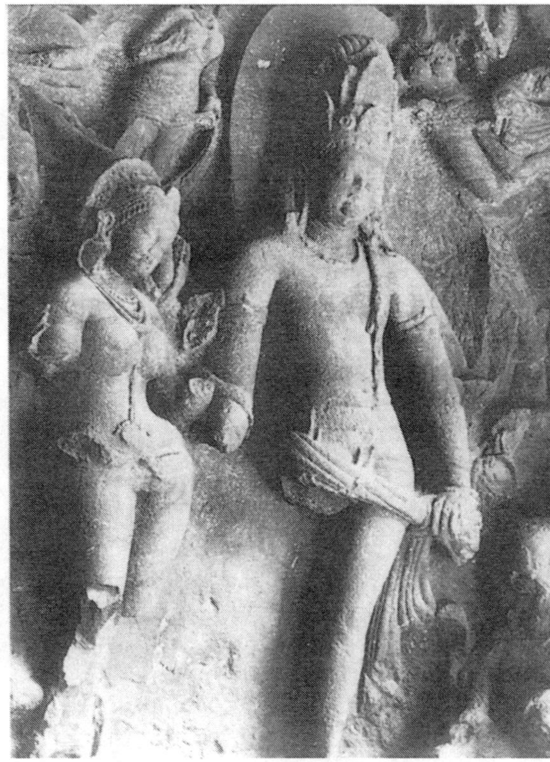

PL. 54. Kalyanasundara—Marriage (of Shiva and Parvati). Parvati and Shiva.

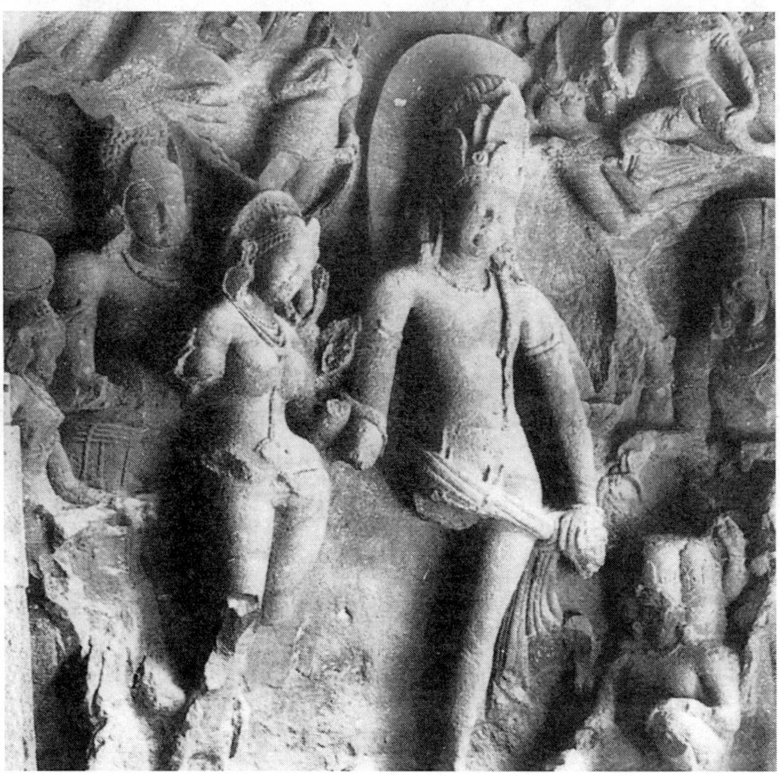

PL. 55. Kalyanasundara—Marriage (of Shiva and Parvati), Himalaya Parvati and Shiva

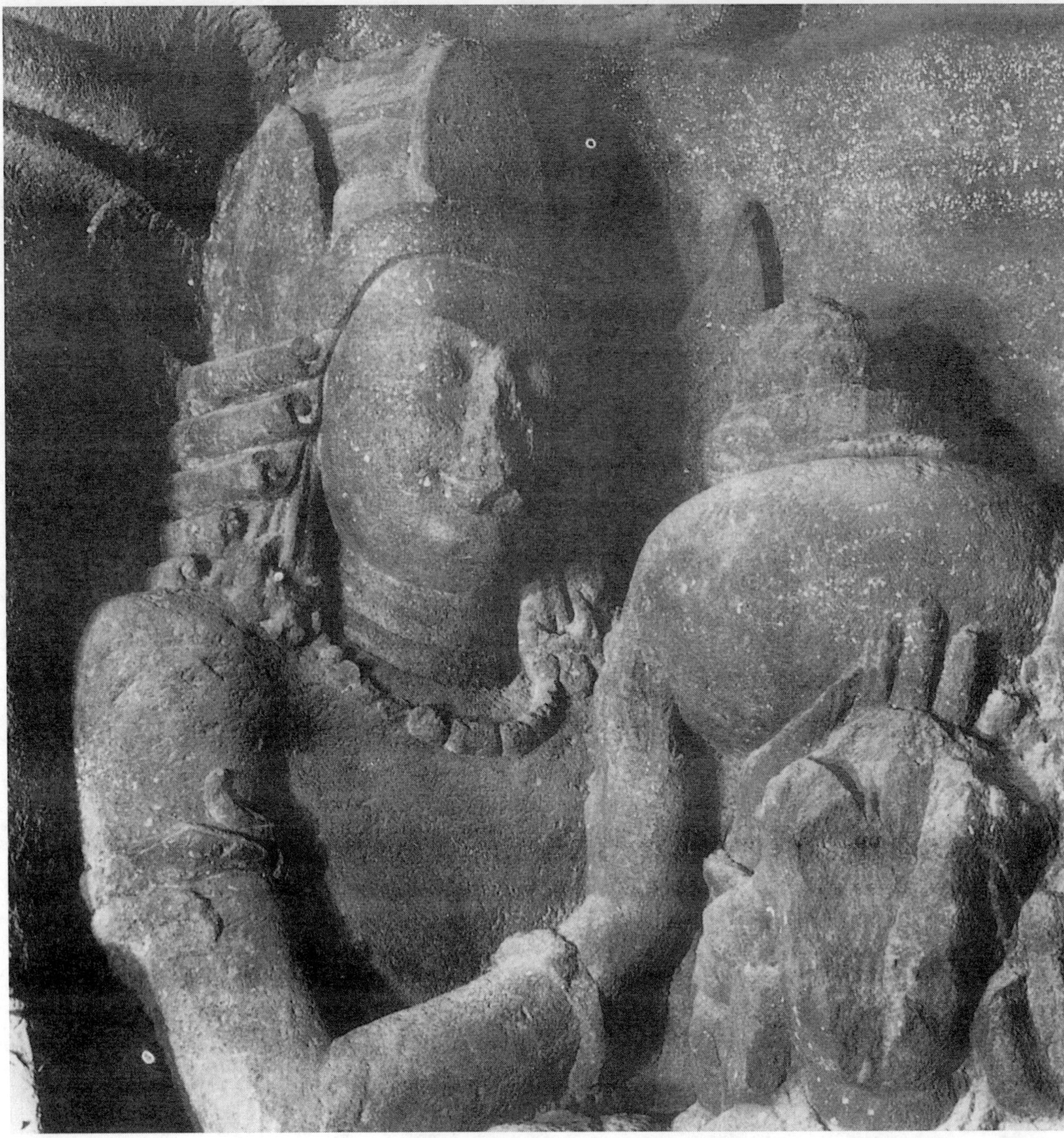

PL. 56. Kalyanasundara—Marriage (of Shiva and Parvati). Candra offering a pot of honey.

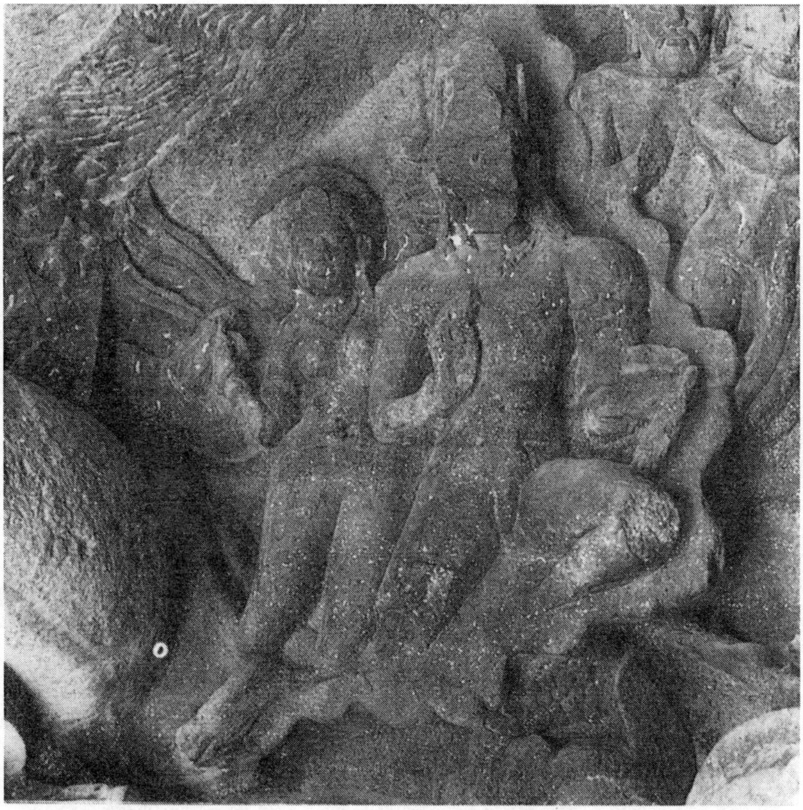

PL. 57. Kalyanasundara—Marriage (of Shiva and Parvati), flying figures.

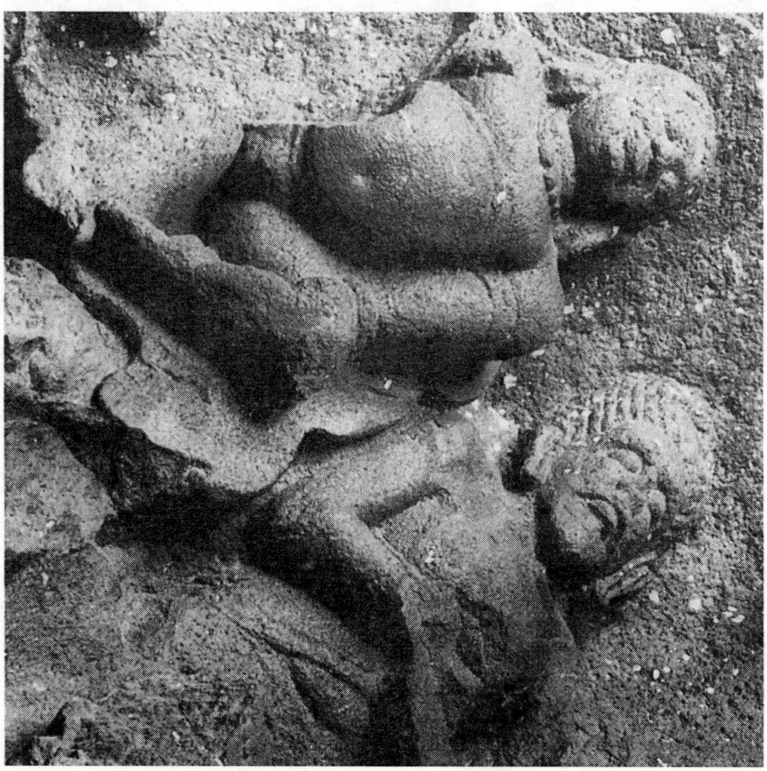

PL. 58. Kalyanasundara—Marriage (of Shiva and Parvati), flying figures.

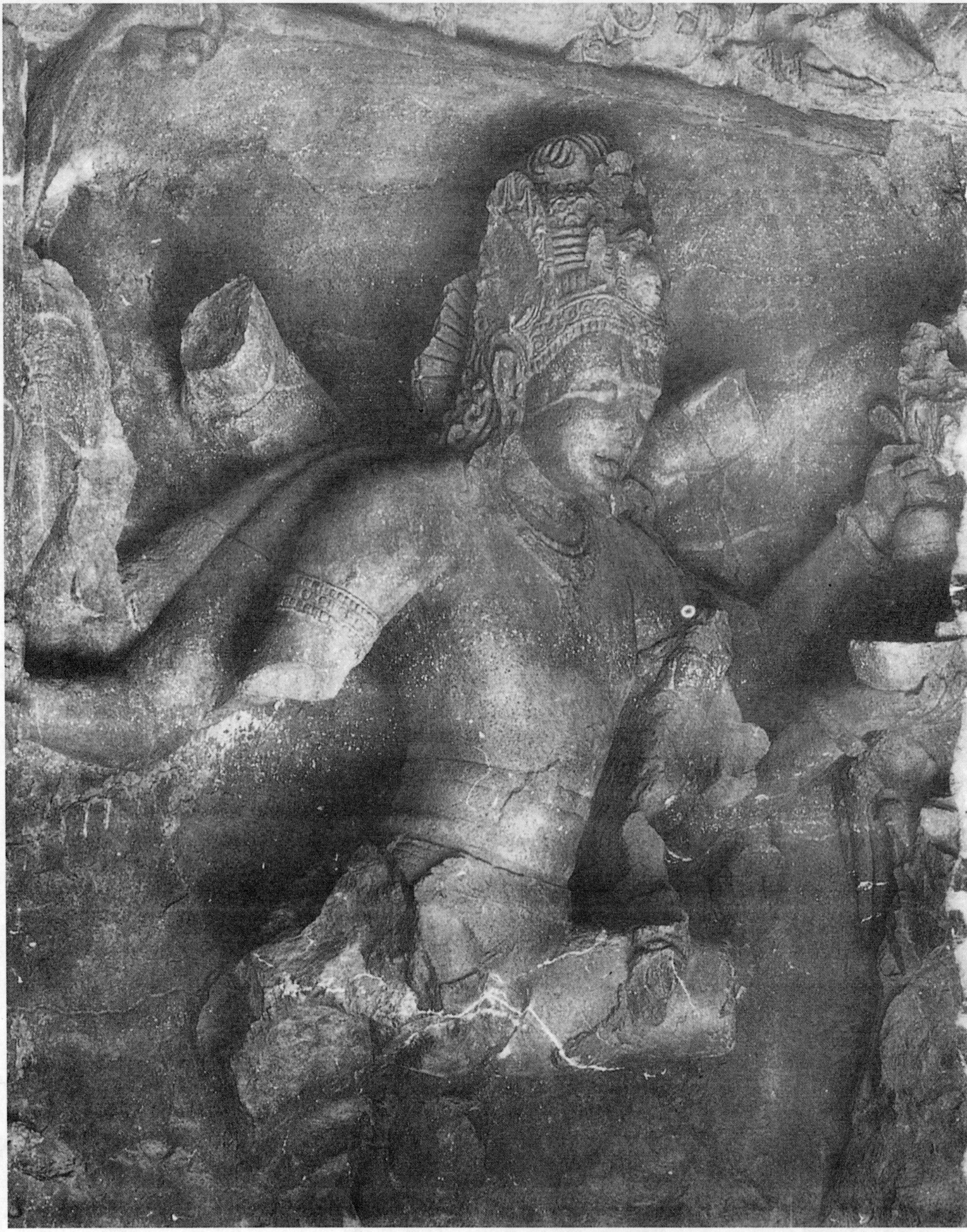

PL. 59. Andhakasuravadha—(Impaling the demon Andhaka), west veranda, north wall.

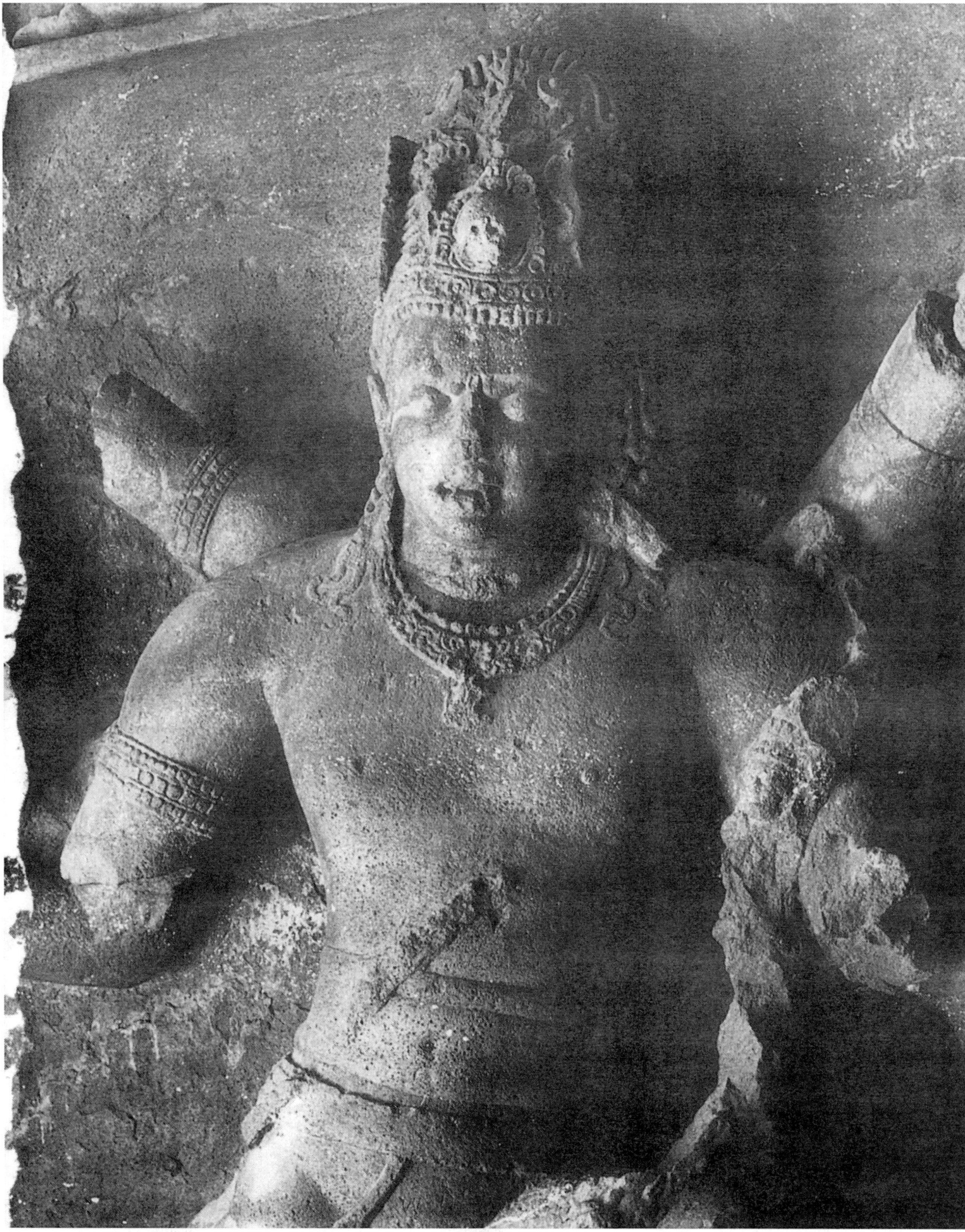

PL. 60. Andhakasuravadha—(Impaling the demon Andhaka), detail.

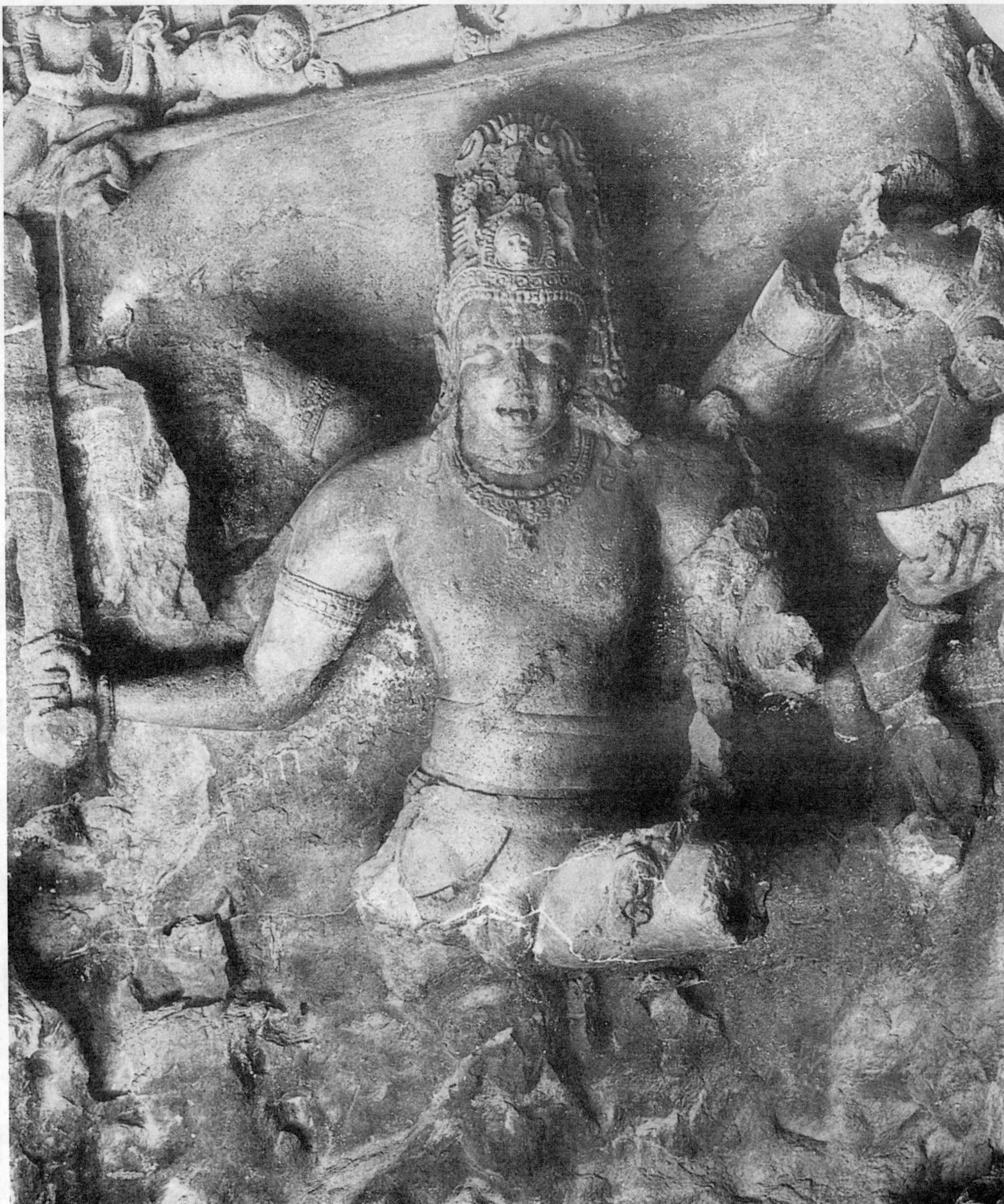

PL. 61. Andhakasuravadha—(Impaling the demon Andhaka), with sword against Nila's head and broken figure of Andhaka at east upper corner.

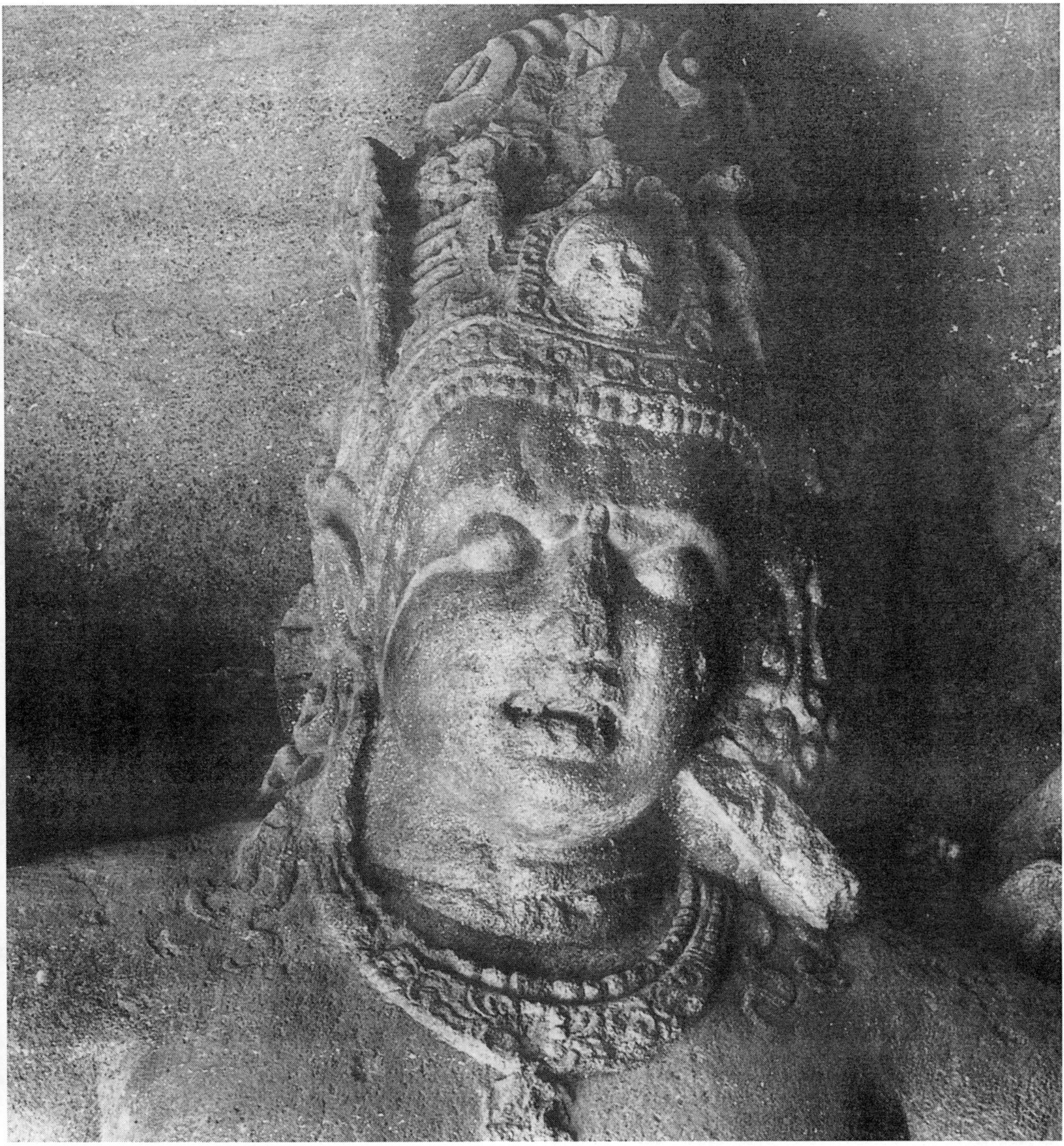

PL. 62. Andhakasuravadha—(Impaling the demon Andhaka); head of Shiva.

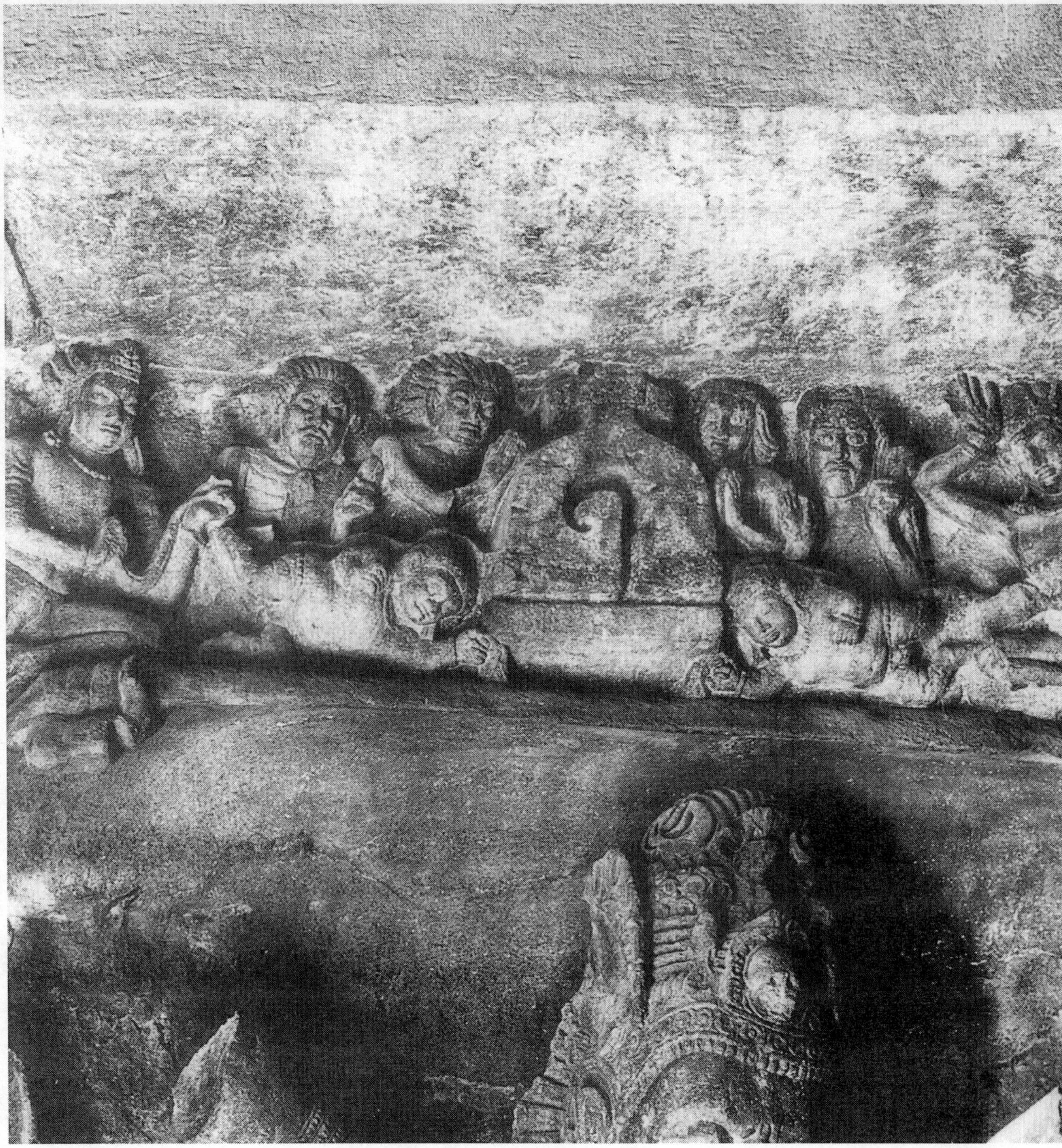

PL. 63. Andhakasuravadha—(Impaling the demon Andhaka), partial view of the lintel.

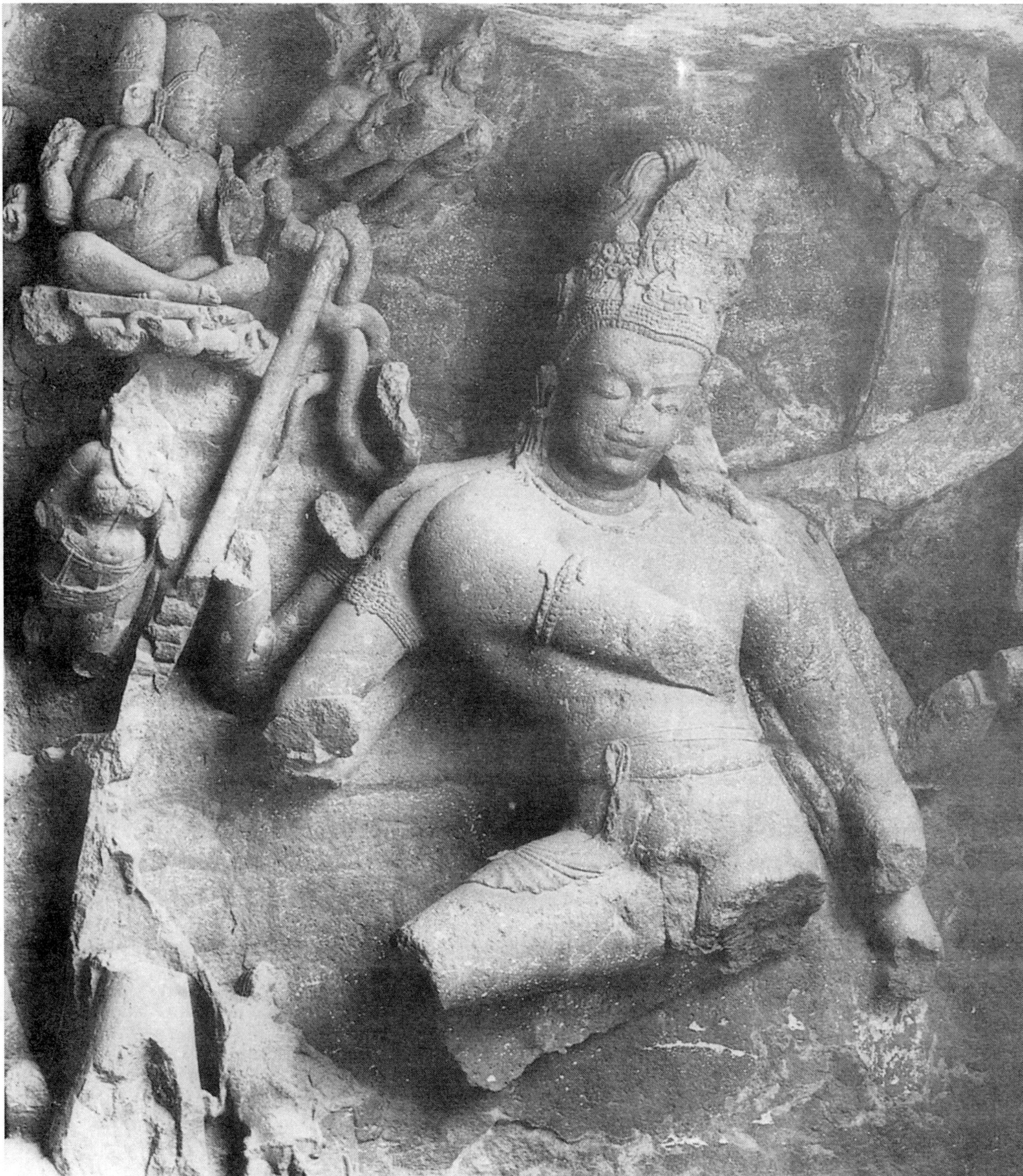

PL. 64. Nataraja—Shiva Dancing (in *Lalita*) panel.

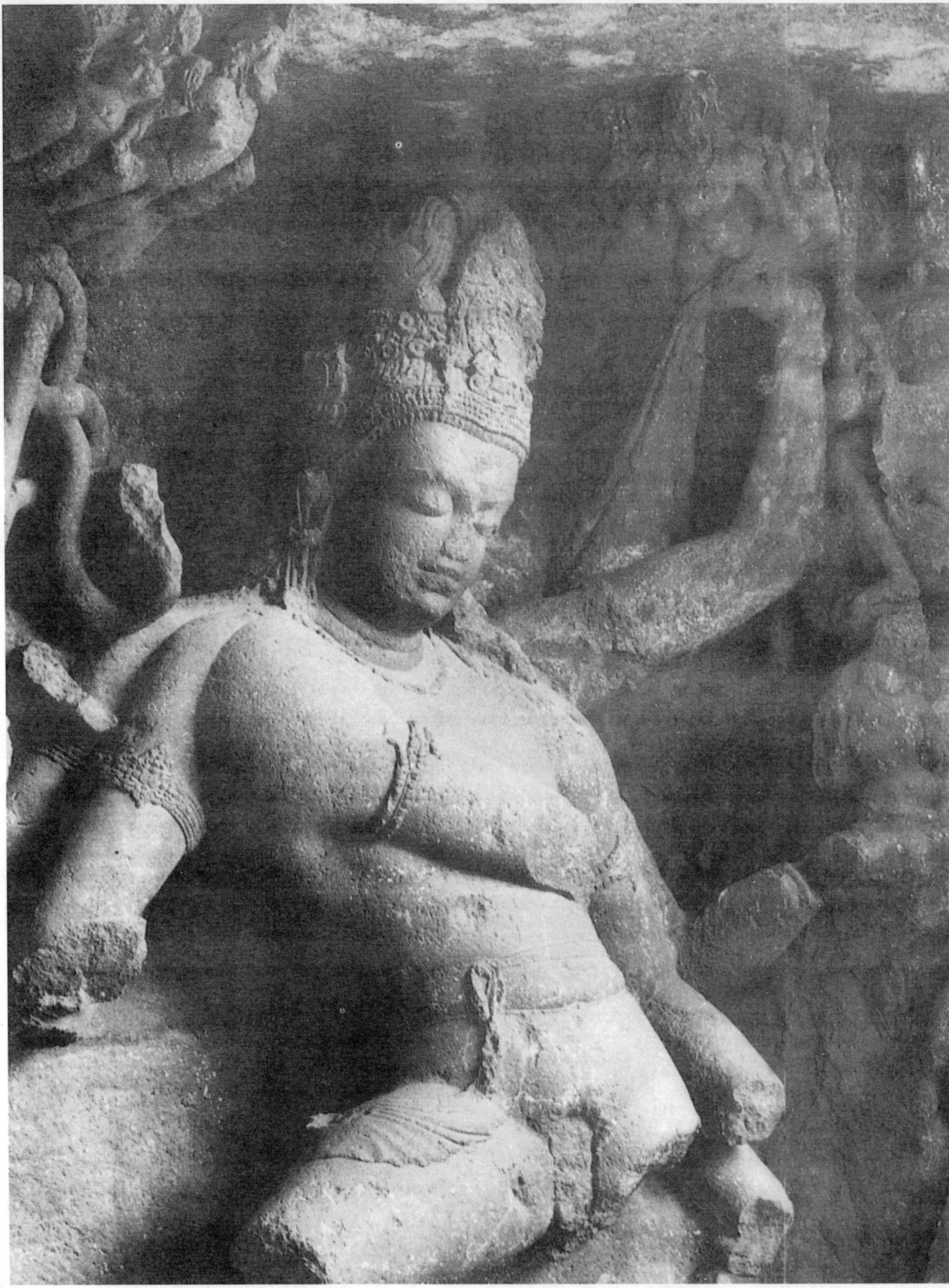

PL. 65. (Opposite) Nataraja—Shiva Dancing (in *Lalita*), Shiva's left arm lifts the veil of illusion.

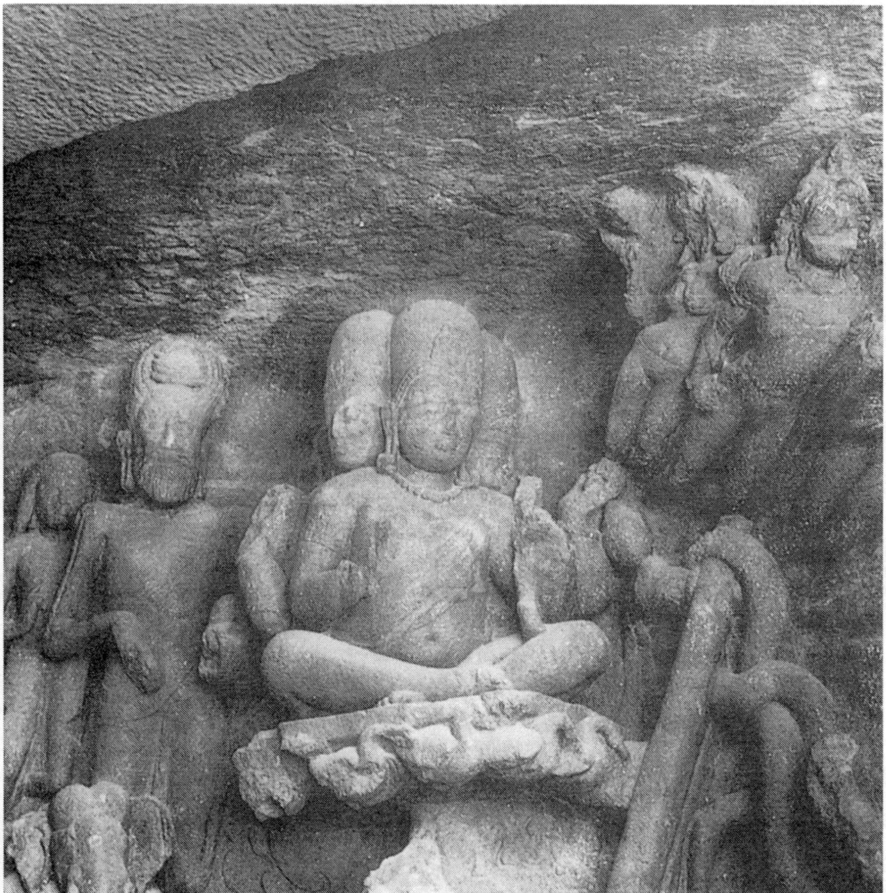

PL. 66. Nataraja—Shiva Dancing (in *Lalita*), Brahma with three visible heads seated on his seat of swans, with worshipers.

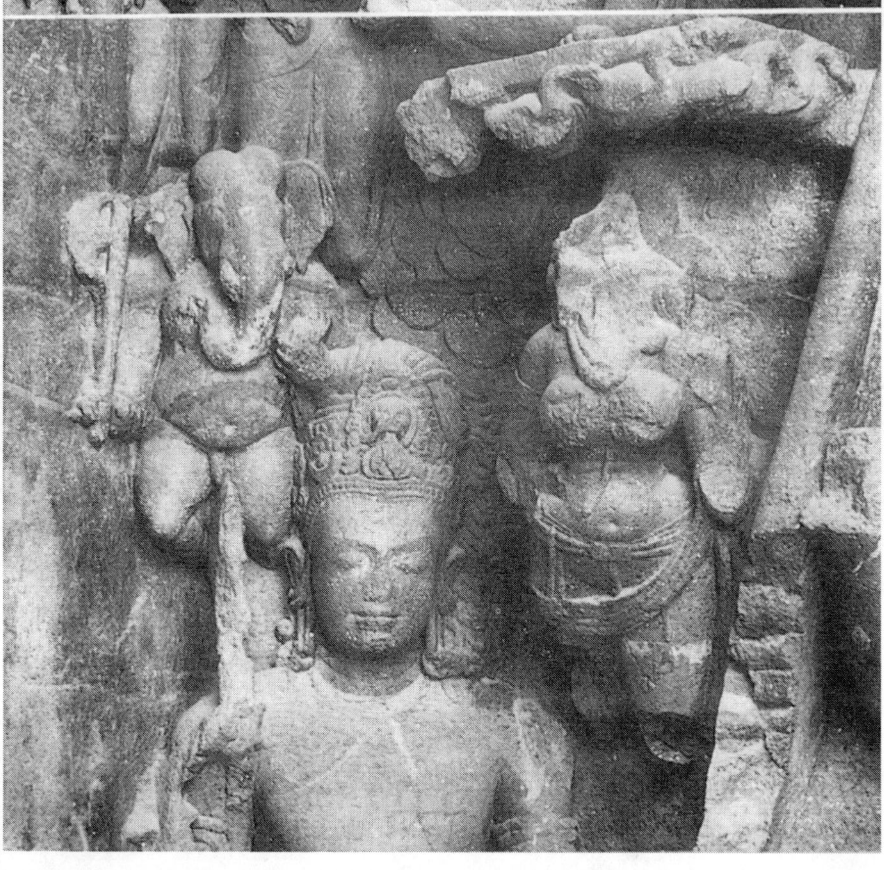

PL. 67. Nataraja—Shiva Dancing (in *Lalita*), Ganesha, Karttikeya and *apsara*.

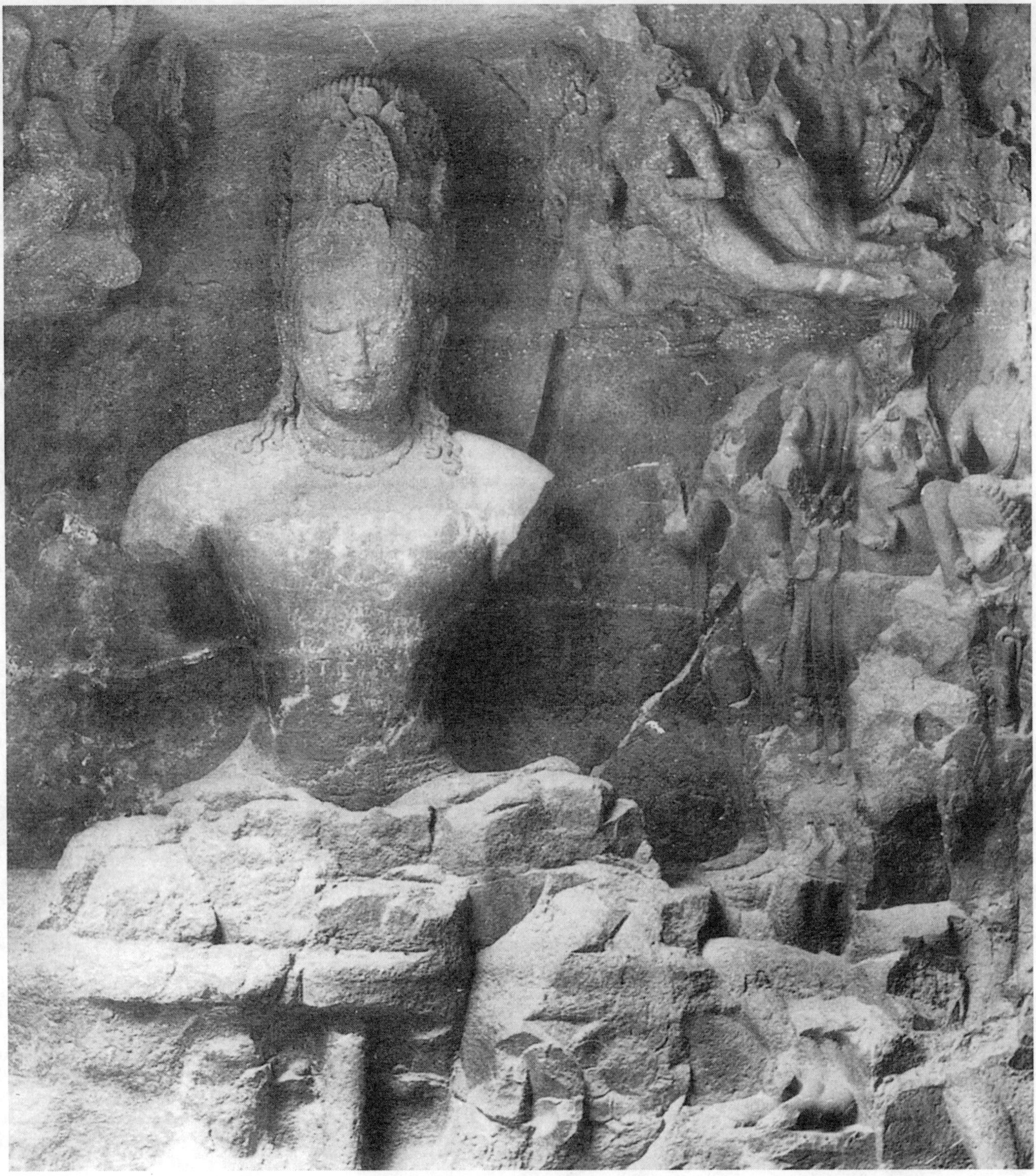

PL. 68. Yogishvara—Lord of Yogis panel.

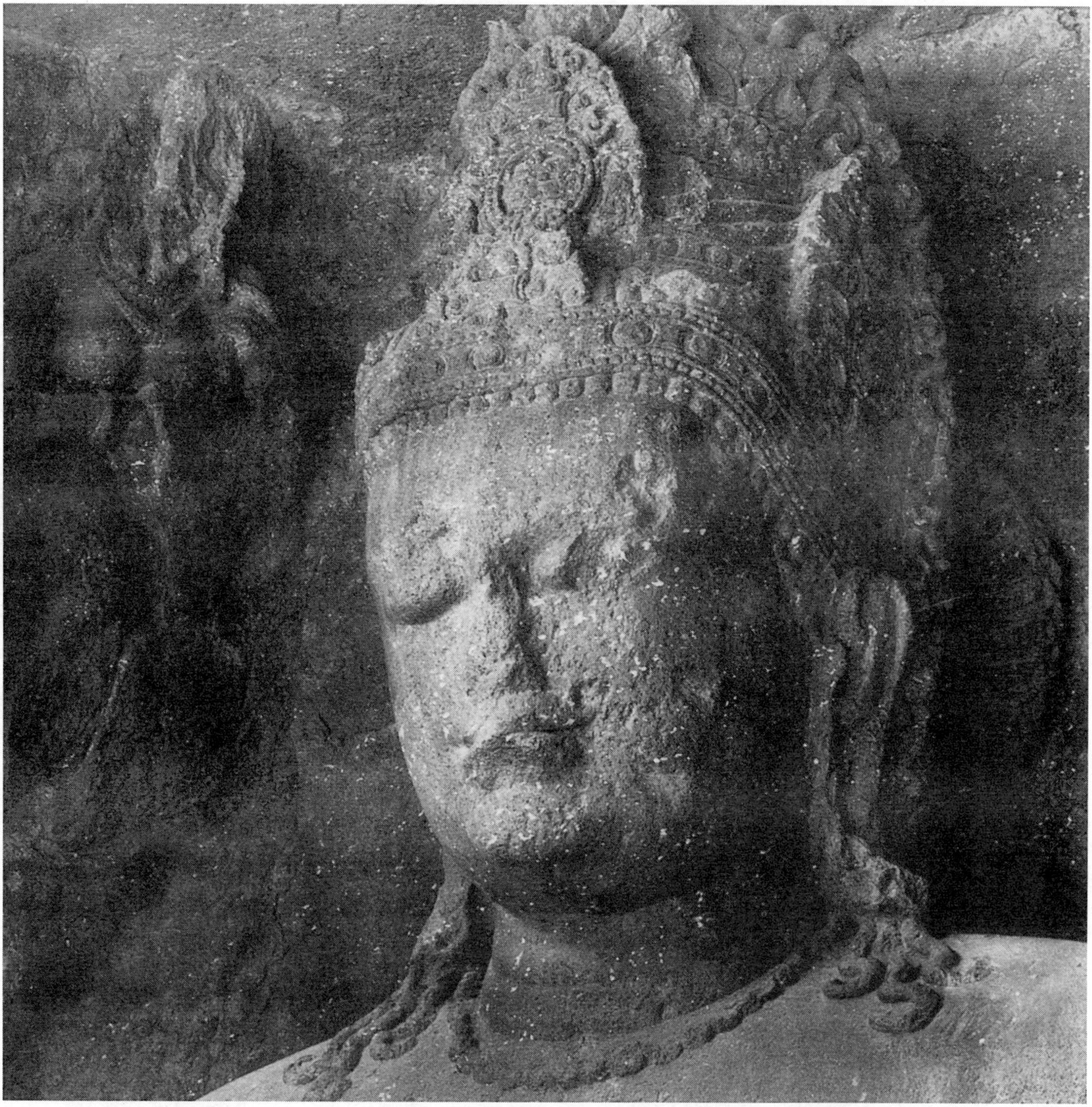

PL. 69. Yogishvara—Lord of Yogis, head of Shiva.

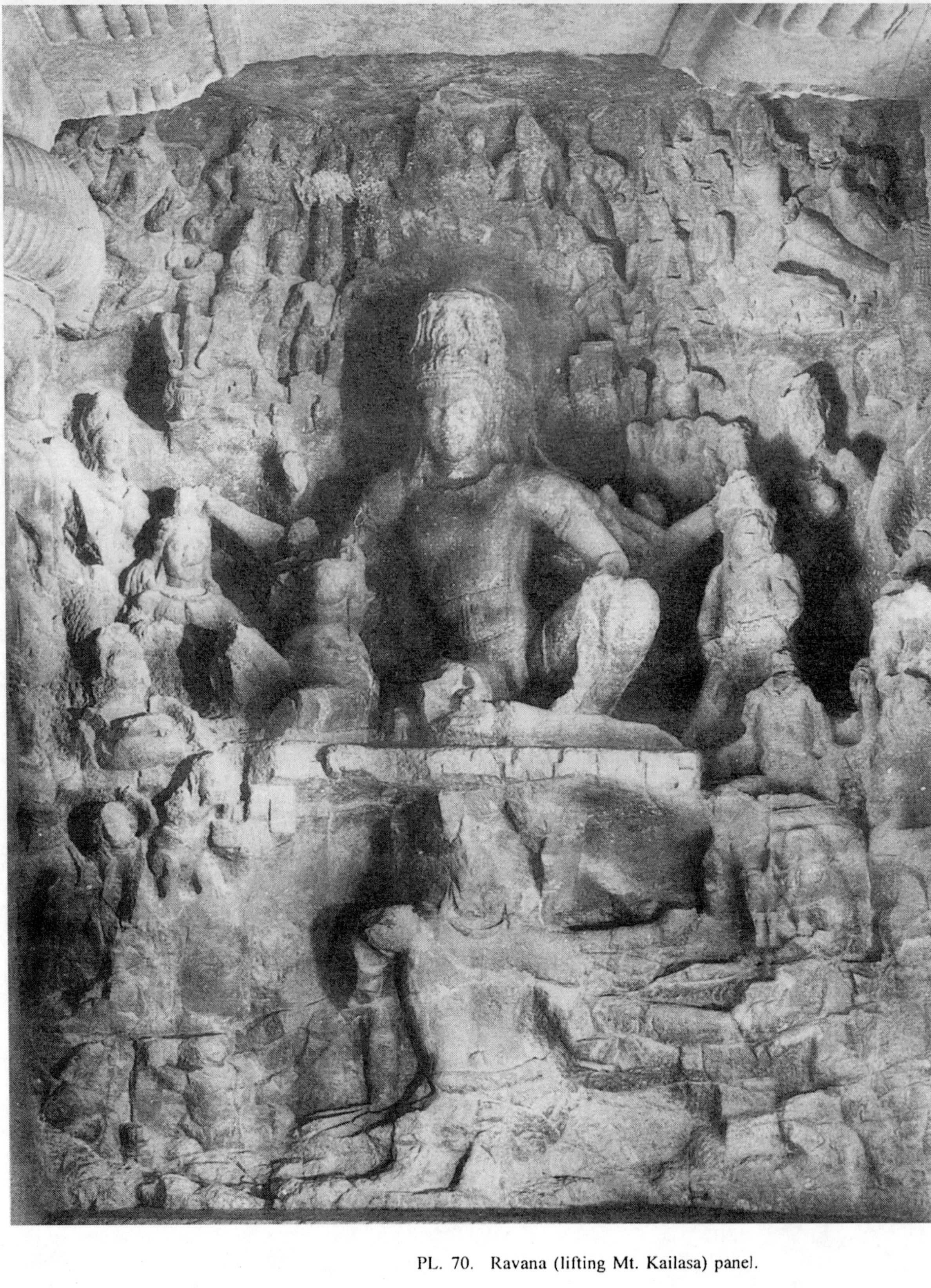

PL. 70. Ravana (lifting Mt. Kailasa) panel.

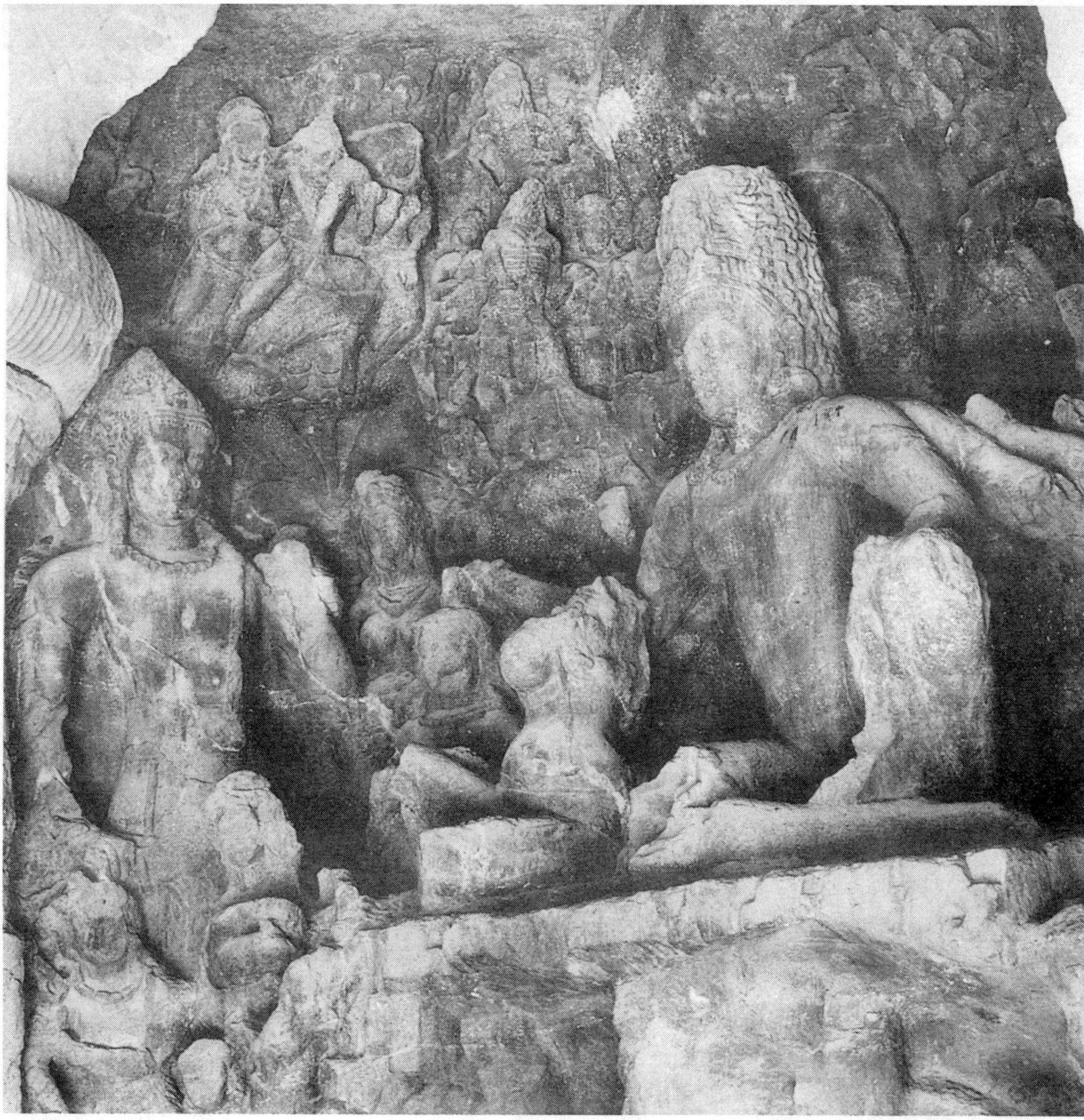

PL. 71. Ravana (lifting Mt. Kailasa), from the east.

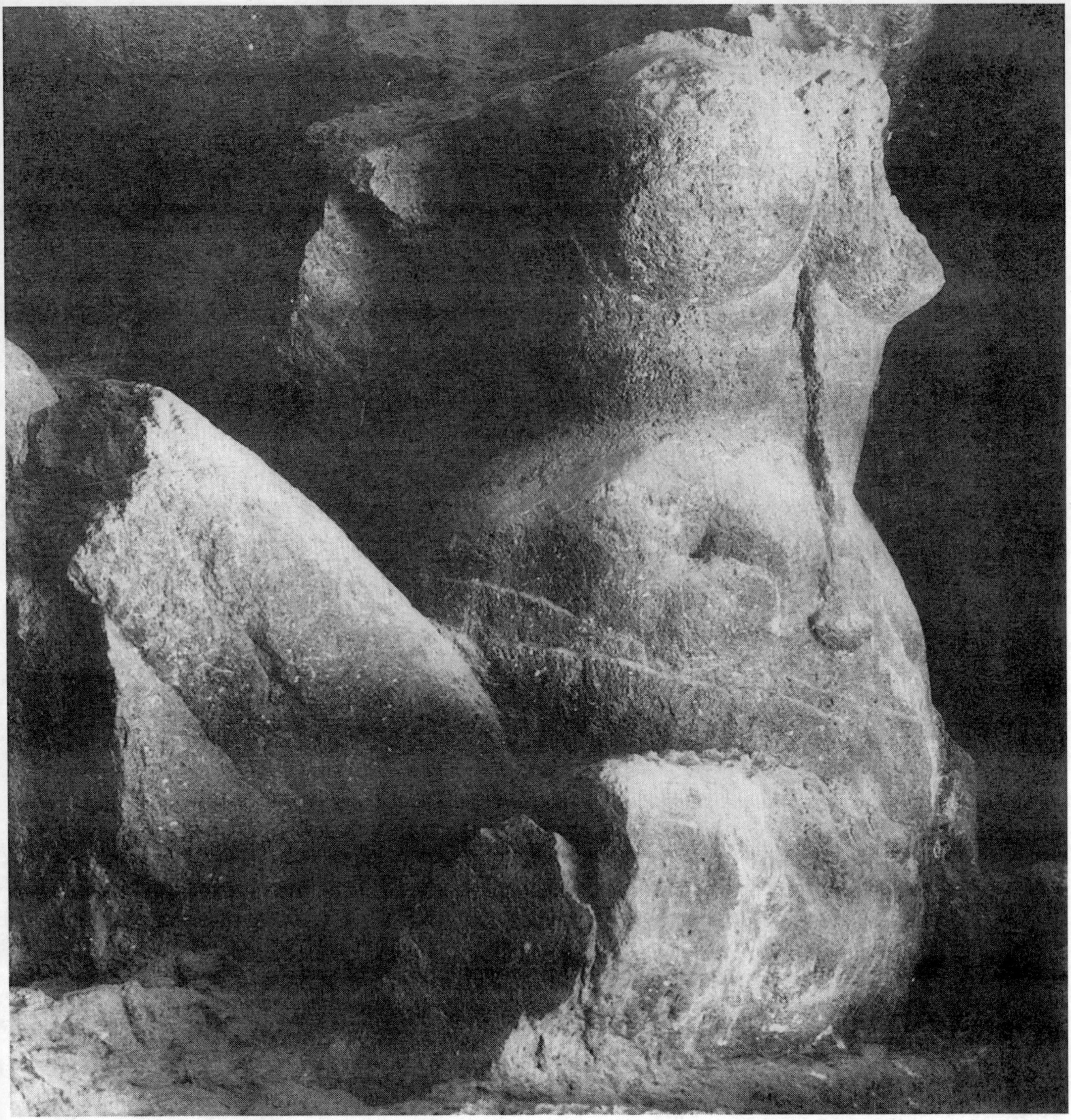

PL. 72. Ravana (lifting Mt. Kailasa), the figure of Parvati.

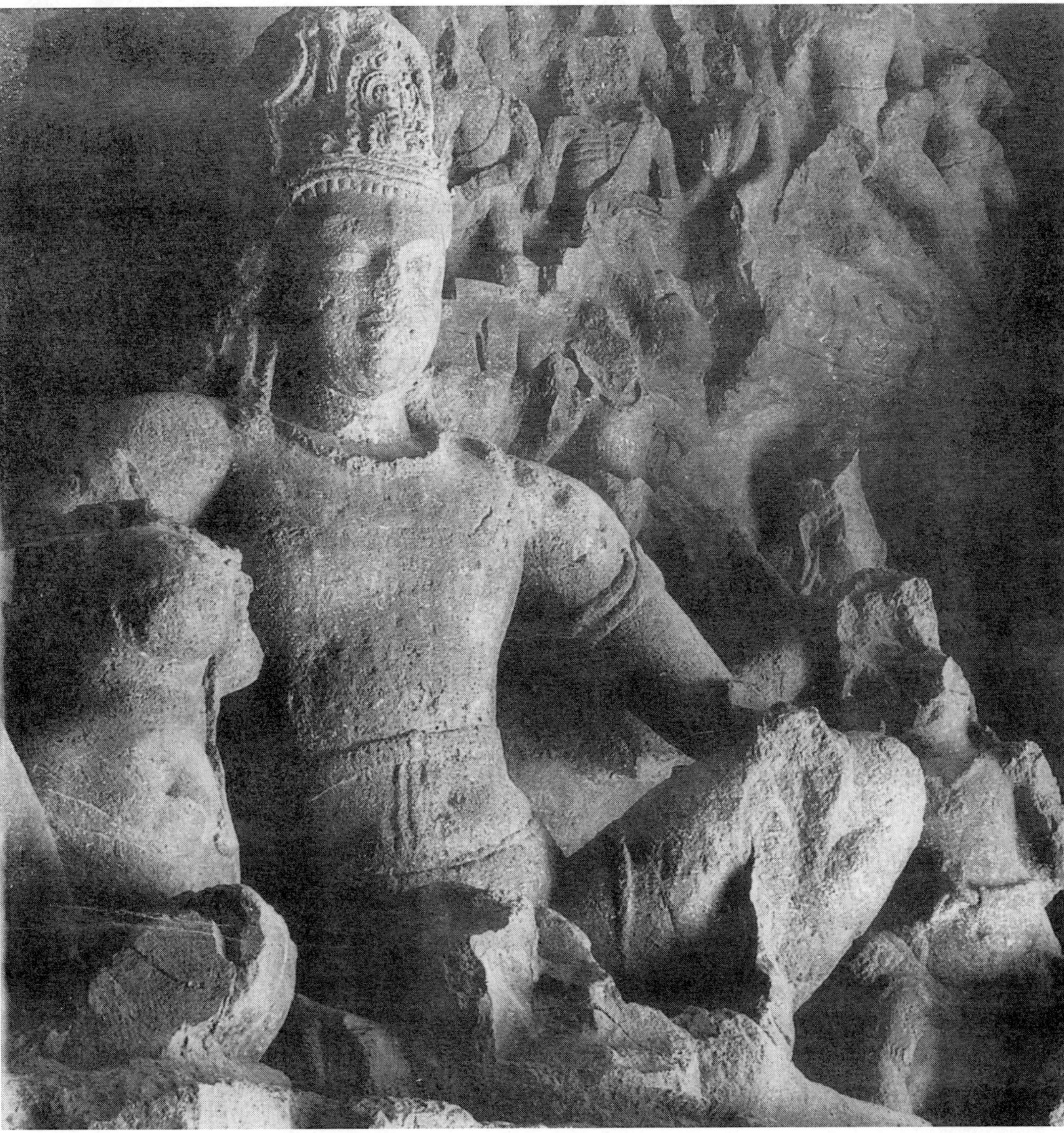

PL. 73. Ravana (lifting Mt. Kailasa), Shiva and Parvati.

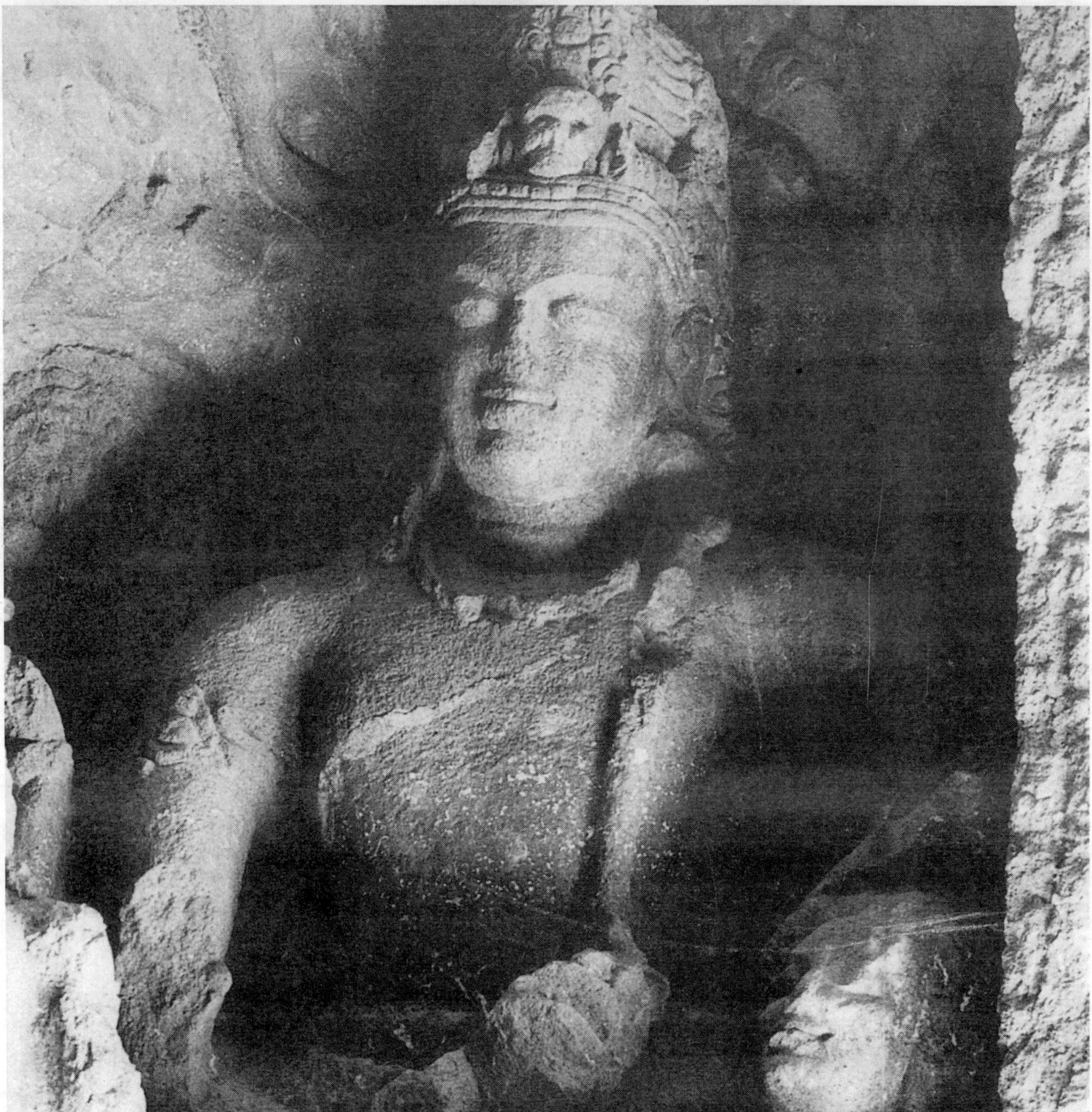

PL. 74. Ravana (lifting Mt. Kailasa), *dvarapala*.